Letters of Advice for Child Care Providers

Letters of Advice for Child Care Providers

Elizabeth Lawson-Lilley
Kathryn Lating-Wise

THOMSON
DELMAR LEARNING

Australia Canada Mexico Singapore Spain United Kingdom United States

THOMSON
DELMAR LEARNING

Letters of Advice for Child Care Providers
by Elizabeth Lawson-Lilley and Kathryn Lating-Wise

Vice President, Career Ed SBU:
Dawn Gerrain

Acquisitions Editor:
Erin O'Connor

Developmental Editor:
Alexis Ferraro

Editorial Assistant:
Ivy Ip

Director of Production:
Wendy A. Troeger

Production Assistant:
Erica Seeley

Director of Marketing:
Donna J. Lewis

Cover Designer
Joseph Villanova

Composition:
Larry O'Brien

Printed in Canada
1 2 3 4 5 XXX 07 06 05 04 03

For more information contact Delmar, 5 Maxwell Drive, Clifton Park, NY 12065-2919 at http://www.EarlyChildEd.delmar.com

Library of Congress Cataloging-in-Publication Data

Lawson-Lilley, Elizabeth.
Letters of advice for child care providers / Elizabeth Lawson-Lilley, Kathryn Lating-Wise.
p. cm.
Includes index.
ISBN 1-4018-3725-5 (alk. paper)
1. Child care workers—United States—Handbooks, manuals, etc. 2. Child care—United States—Handbooks, manuals, etc. I. Lating-Wise, Kathryn. II. Title.
HQ778.63.L38 2003
362.71'2'0973—dc22

2003053371

Contents

An Opening Word

This book is intended to serve as a manual for parents and child care providers alike. Because child-rearing is primarily a matter of trial and error, we decided to compile an analysis of some real-life experiences in the hope that you will gain knowledge and be enlightened!

I, Kathy—a mother of one—am a licensed child care provider in the state of Maryland. My home child care opened on August 11, 1997. At the present time, I share my home with several wonderful children ranging in age from six weeks to nine years. My day begins at 6:45 in the morning. The day ends at 5:30 in the evening. My license permits up to eight children in my home at one time. In accordance with this requirement, I offer before and after school child care, as well as full- and part-time child care.

I try to approach each day in a positive manner. Over the past four years, I kept a diary of the challenges that I encountered throughout the day. When time permitted, I would present my journal to my close friend, Libby, who is a pediatric nurse practitioner. She would review the journal and offer advice.

Libby is a 1974 graduate of the Nurse Practitioner Program at Johns Hopkins School of Health and Hygiene. As a nurse practitioner, she is trained in health care, which includes growth and development as well as social and behavior issues. Nurse practitioners are another type of provider—similar to pediatricians; they perform physicals as well as diagnose, treat, and prescribe for illnesses. She was the first nurse practitioner in the state of Maryland to own and manage her own pediatric primary care center. Libby is the mother of two grown sons and two stepdaughters. She has over 25 years of experience in the health field and as a parent.

This book, arranged in an easy-to-read question-and-answer format, reflects situations encountered by parents and a child care provider over many years. The situations presented in these letters actually happened. However, names have been changed to respect the children's privacy. Although the actual setting for these scenarios was a home child care environment, the situations represent common concerns for parents and caregivers in any setting. Our questions and answers follow the rules and regulations in force in the state of Maryland. Make sure that you refer to your state's guidelines pertaining to child care environments before acting according to any of our suggestions.

Acknowledgments

Elizabeth Lawson-Lilley

This book is dedicated to my husband Robert for his patience and unconditional love, and to my children Robin, Nathan, Shanna, and Brandon for growing into responsible and happy adults.

I wish to thank my patients and their parents for allowing me the chance to watch their children grow and develop. A heartfelt thank you to ALL my patients, whose lives have touched mine forever.

A special thank you to Jinae Lawson for typing the entire first draft and to Dean Johnson for helping me with computer skills and helping us meet deadlines.

Kathryn Lating-Wise

This book is dedicated to my mother and father for always believing in me, to my wonderful husband Jerry for all his love and support, and to my beautiful angel Alexandra—I love you!

I wish to express my appreciation to the child care parents who allowed me the opportunity to share in their children's lives, and to the wonderful children who fill my day with laughter and love.

I would also like to extend a special thank you to Natalie Danish for her assistance with all my computer needs and to Jerry Wise for his countless hours of proofreading. Special thanks to Alex for showing me how to cut and paste.

We both would like to thank Ivy Ip for all her guidance and support.

We are also grateful to the following reviewers, enlisted by Delmar Learning, for their helpful suggestions and constructive criticism:

Billie Armstrong
Tyrrell County Head Start
Columbia, NC

Victoria Folds, Ed.D.
Tutor Time Learning Systems
Boca Raton, FL

Sandra Hughes
Rainbow Express Child Care Center
Schenectady, NY

Jody Martin
Children's World Learning Centers
Golden, CO

Brenda Schin
Private Child Care Provider
Selkirk, NY

Chapter 1

LETTERS ON HEALTH

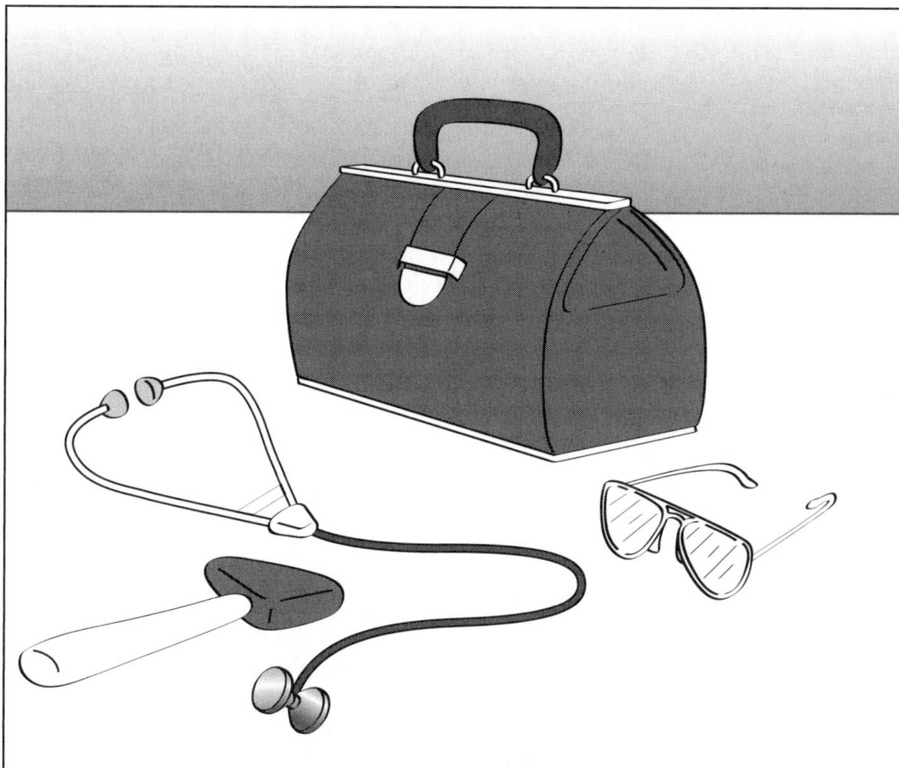

Bowel Habits

Q

Dear Nurse Libby,

One of my toddler's parents just had a baby girl. The mother has discussed with me her concerns that the baby is three weeks old and screams constantly. The mother states that the infant is constipated and that Mom has tried everything to help her baby. She finally took the baby to the doctor because she was concerned about the screaming. She stated that the baby had a terrible diaper rash and wondered if this had anything to do with the screaming. The doctor told Ricky's mom that the rash is the reason that the baby is constipated. He explained that the baby realized that every time she had a bowel movement it would hurt, so she had tightened her muscles so much for fear of pain that now she cannot go. He told her that she should not touch the baby's bottom at all so that the muscles would start to relax. He told Mom that if the baby had a bowel movement, she should run baby's bottom under warm water and let her air-dry. It has been over one week, and the baby is still screaming and constipated.

A

Dear Mrs. Kathy,

Infant's bowel habits vary greatly. One infant can have a stool after every feeding, whereas another infant can have only one stool every three days. All infants look like they are having a hard time when they have their bowel movements. Their nervous system is immature, causing them to bear down, turn red, and sometimes cry when they pass a stool. By the time they are three months old, they have a mature nervous system, and they will no longer act this way. The consistency of the stool defines constipation. If the stool is soft and seedy then it is not constipation. If it is hard and dry, that is true constipation.

If, indeed, this infant has not had a bowel movement in a week, it is constipation. Some infants cannot tolerate cow's milk, which is the base for our most commonly used formulas. She should be given a trial on soy-based or lactose-free formulas to find one she can tolerate.

Infants usually do not remember pain so well as to consciously tighten her muscles in fear of the pain. Maybe the mom misunderstood what the doctor was explaining to her. The treatment for the diaper rash, especially after a bowel movement, is an acceptable one.

In any case, this infant needs re-evaluation for the cause and treatment of not having a bowel movement in a week!

Q

Dear Nurse Libby,

Yesterday Paul (15 months) had three loose stools that were yellow in color. The last stool was all mucus. What would cause this? Is it something to worry about?

A

Dear Mrs. Kathy,

Yes, yellow stools with mucus are something to worry about. It is a sign of not digesting food properly. The reasons for this could be simply a viral infection or something more serious, such as a malabsorption problem. If the occurrence is limited to three stools in only one day, the reason was probably a virus—one, by the way, that Paul was able to handle pretty well. The only thing to do would be to give him a bland diet—for example, the BRAT diet of *B*ananas, *R*ice, *A*pplesauce, and *T*oast—for a day or two to allow his digestive tract to heal from the virus. These intestinal viruses are highly contagious! So, if you allow him to be at the child care center, you must use good hand-washing technique before and after caring for him, and do not let any of the other children share drinks and food with him. (I'm sure that you discourage this behavior anyway, but we all know how toddlers can be!)

If, on the other hand, this is persistent for more than six stools in twenty-four hours and/or lasts more than twenty-four hours, his primary care provider should evaluate him. He would at least need to be weighed and re-evaluated, possibly have some stool cultures done, and have his diet modified.

Hopefully, it was a virus that Paul was able to handle pretty well.

Q

Dear Nurse Libby,

Paul (age 16 months) went to his primary care provider for diarrhea that continued on and off for four weeks. The doctor stated that the diarrhea was caused by him drinking 2% milk, not whole milk. Is this true? What are the guidelines for milk with children?

A

Dear Mrs. Kathy,

The guideline for milk with children is whole milk until the age of two. The most important reason for this is proper brain development. When the fat is cut in milk, as in the case of 2% milk and the other low-fat milks, the protein is changed. Children, under the age of two years, are still developing their brain. Protein is needed in this development. Toddlers, although they are drinking much less milk than infants, get much of this protein from milk.

Some toddlers can also have digestive, malabsorption problems when they are given less than whole milk. Diarrhea is a common sign of these occurrences. So, for all these reasons, especially brain development, keep all children on whole milk until two years of age.

Illness

Q

Dear Nurse Libby,

One of the most difficult decisions that I am faced with is trying to determine whether a child should not be permitted into the child care center due to illness. What guidelines should I follow? For example,

- *fever—at what temperature should the child remain at home? How long after the fever breaks can the child return to the child care center?*
- *vomiting—how long should a child remain home after vomiting episodes?*
- *diarrhea—please describe what you consider diarrhea to be—for example, the number of movements and type.*
- *runny nose—what if the discharge is clear? yellow or green?*
- *cough—do different guidelines apply to dry hacking cough, productive cough, and the crouplike cough?*
- *rash—some rashes are itchy, irritated skin; some have bumps, raised or under the skin. How do I respond in each case?*

I normally recommend that parents have a backup plan available so that if a child is too sick to attend school or child care, a family member or a close friend can come to the home to stay with the child. What would you recommend?

A

Dear Mrs. Kathy,

Young children are usually sick, more often, with minor illnesses as they build up their immune system. A child care center is a place where young children are in close proximity to one another. They will be passing viruses and bacterial infections back and forth, as if they are in school. The best way to help keep these infections to a minimum is good hand-washing between the intimate care of sick children, which I'm sure you are doing. Another measure is to be sure that the child care center has a good ventilation system in the building. A third consideration, one that many people may not be aware of, is that the children need to get outside everyday, even in the winter. Fresh air and sunshine are natural immune-system builders. Even in the winter be sure to apply sunscreen to all exposed areas. Of course good sense needs to prevail concerning rainy days, heavy snowfalls, and severe temperatures. Severe temperature good sense should prevail in hot, humid, or dry climates, also.

Now to specifically address your concerns for when to keep a sick child at home:

- **Fever**—a child with a fever over 101°F is fighting an infection. The child's resistance is down already. If exposed to more infections, the child could become sicker. Therefore, for the sick child's well-being as well as that of the other children, that child should remain home until the fever is below 101°F for twenty-four hours.

- **Vomiting**—this issue is not cut and dry. If a child vomits only once, in the early morning, and has no fever, that child can attend the child care center. You should adjust the diet though. Use the BRAT diet (i.e., bananas, rice, applesauce, and toast)—anything bland, no dairy products, and no caffeine. If a child has vomited more than once and/or has a fever over 101°F, that child needs to stay home until that magical twenty-four hours is up! This again, is to help the child recover more quickly and not expose the other children.

- **Diarrhea**—the typical description of diarrhea is at least six loose watery stools in a twenty-four-hour period. If a child meets those criteria, that child should not be at a child care center. If the child has one or two soft or loose stools (not meeting the given criteria), that child should be allowed to attend the child care center. You can help them by adjusting their diet to the BRAT/bland diet. Obviously, good hand-washing technique and measures to disinfect surfaces in the child care center should be conscientiously observed. Soapy water and/or a commercial product of ¼ cup of bleach to 1 gallon of water mixed in a spray bottle will help to prevent contamination to other children. This procedure should be done by the caregiver. Make sure to follow your state regulations for disinfecting your home or center.

- **Runny nose**—did you ever notice that most kindergarten teachers ask each child to bring in a box of tissue for the year? I'm sure that most of those boxes get used during the year. Most preschool age and primary grade students will have an upper respiratory infection at least once a year. This is the common cold. If the discharge is clear and/or yellow, the cause is usually viral. As long as the child does not have a fever, is not vomiting, or does not have diarrhea, that child should be allowed to attend child care. A child who has a green or heavy nasal discharge should be evaluated by the primary care provider to discern whether there is a bacterial reason for the runny nose. Even so, after treatment is started, and as long as there is no fever or severe diarrhea or vomiting, the child should be allowed to attend the child care center.

- **Cough**—the common cold can cause this symptom. The dry hacking cough is relieved with cough suppressants and humidity, which should be administered at home. A cold, with this type of cough, could be the only symptom and could last a week to ten days. Any persistent cough lasting ten or more days should be evaluated by a health care provider.

  The productive cough is a cough in which the child actually produces phlegm. As long as the mucus/phlegm is clear and the child has no fever or other symptoms, this is probably a virus. If, however, the mucus/phlegm is thick, yellow, or green and a fever develops, the child should not attend child care until a health care provider evaluates the child.

  Another type of cough is a wet sounding (moist) nonproductive cough. This cough could be a symptom of a lung or bronchial infection. This child should also be evaluated before attending school or child care.

  To repeat: The spread of infection to the other children and child care providers can be limited by frequent and proper hand-washing techniques as well as disinfecting common surfaces.

- **Rashes**—rashes cannot be diagnosed without being seen. It is probably a good rule to insist that children with a rash be evaluated by their primary care provider before being allowed to attend child care. Most rashes are of viral origin, are self-limiting, and resolve without treatment, but a child with a rash still should be diagnosed prior to attending child care.

Q

Dear Nurse Libby,

I have always heard that being properly dressed for the winter helps prevent certain illnesses. Is this true?

A

Dear Mrs. Kathy,

To answer your question scientifically, I would have to say no. Viruses don't care whether a person is bundled up, has a dry head, or took a bath in the morning right before going out in the cold! (These are some other known, nonscientific reasons for people getting sick.) The reason we get sick, or catch a virus, is that our individual immune system is not resistant to the particular virus. Viruses are also very smart! They can change their construction so that when we do build up resistance to a particular strain, they are no longer that strain and they can attack our immune system again and again!

So, the way we fight viruses is to keep our immune system as fit as we can. We do this by getting proper nutrients, adequate rest, and normal exercise—all the good things we are hearing about for fighting any disease! We ideally should dress for the temperature, not for the season. We want our body temperature to be as close to normal as possible. When we become either overheated or chilled, our body works overtime to regulate our temperature. This "overworking" brings our body's resistance down and increases our susceptibility to outside influence, meaning the virus of the day! This explains why people who get soaked in a rainstorm, for instance, and don't dry off right away tend to catch a cold soon thereafter.

Children are naturally more susceptible to viruses, as they are building up their immune systems with each new virus they are exposed to. By the time children are about twelve years old, their immune systems should be pretty well developed. That is why most of the time, the younger child will be sicker and will be sick more often!

Q

Dear Nurse Libby,

Yesterday, Jenny (age 3½) woke up from an afternoon nap in a full-blown asthma attack. She was diagnosed with asthma when she was 2 years old. I did have an inhaler that I gave her to try to improve her breathing. It unfortunately did not work. It also happened to be her mother's first day on her new job and I could not reach her at work. Nor could I reach anyone at the emergency contact number for Jenny. Please offer some suggestions about what I could have done to comfort Jenny. Also, how would I know when she needs to get to a hospital? I would like to add that her mother did take Jenny to the emergency room and she was admitted.

A

Dear Mrs. Kathy,

As you found out, an asthma attack is a scary thing—it can be life threatening. I'm assuming that the inhaler you gave Jenny was prescribed for her. Hopefully, it was a short acting one (which means it acts quickly). Most children her age, though, cannot inhale the medication to properly get it into their lungs. As you found out, it did little to help her respiratory problems. Because you describe no other medications, I am assuming that Jenny doesn't experience this very often, nor is she on medications on a regular basis. Therefore, I will suggest first-aid kinds of remedies.

The BEST thing to help an asthma attack, especially if you have no other medications, is intense humidity. If you have a humidifier, fill it with water only. You could set it up so that the mist blows in Jenny's face. She would then breathe it in to her lungs, helping to break up the mucus. If you have no humidifier, take her into the bathroom. Turn on the shower and get the room all steamy. Stay in there with her for about ten minutes. This intense humidity will help break up the mucus. Pay attention to her breathing. If she starts to grunt and/or use her stomach muscles to breathe, call 911!

A child who has been diagnosed as asthmatic may have regular medications. Sometimes, the child is on medications only if actually symptomatic. The use of inhalers is very common. However, because a younger child doesn't always use an inhaler properly, they are sometimes given an air chamber device that helps to get the medication into the lungs easier. Prednisone, an anti-inflammatory medication, is frequently used on young children to help break up the mucus. You would know about these medications for a child with chronic asthma. You would have written permission from the parent and prescribing provider to administer these medications.

However, in your situation as a child care provider, you may witness their first severe attack. In wintertime, a horrible virus called RSV causes bronchiolitis in young children. The symptoms are similar to asthma. If you are the first caregiver to witness a child wheezing, coughing (sometimes with spasms), and/or having difficulty breathing, you need to have a plan of care in place. Obviously, if the child is in distress, call 911 first and then the parent or emergency contact person as soon as possible. If you are the only caregiver in the child care center, you need to designate a backup person—possibly a neighbor or relative—to attend to the other children if you are the one accompanying the child to the hospital. This person or persons has to be approved by your state agency as a backup child care provider. If the child is wheezing for the first time, and is breathing normally, you would notify the parent/emergency contact person and together decide on whether the parent should come and take the child to be medically evaluated.

Rashes

Q

Dear Nurse Libby,

On Sunday, Juan (age four years) had a deer tick on his arm. His mother removed the tick. She then contacted her health care provider to see what to do. They instructed her to bring Juan and the tick in to discuss Lyme disease. Could you please explain what Lyme disease is? What are the signs, symptoms, and the method of treatment? I have now made checking each child from head to toe a part of my daily routine after outside play. Is there anything else I can do?

A

Dear Mrs. Kathy,

This is an important subject. I will answer one question at a time! Lyme disease is an infection that is caused by *Borrelia burgdorferi*, a bacterium that is transmitted to humans by a certain type of tick bite. There are two types of ticks that transmit Lyme disease. The most common one is called the deer tick and is usually found in the northeastern and north-central United States. The western black-legged tick is the carrier on the Pacific Coast of the United States. The name Lyme comes from the town of Lyme, Connecticut, where, in 1977, the bacteria and its route of travel by the ticks was first discovered. These ticks are hard to see. They are much smaller than the common dog and cattle ticks. Their young ticks are no bigger than a pinhead! The adult tick is only approximately $^{2}/_{10}$ to $^{3}/_{10}$ centimeter, or $^{1}/_{8}$ of an inch!!! As you can see, just finding a tick is hard.

The answer to your second question is a little involved. The signs and symptoms of Lyme disease are pretty simple, yet complicated! Let me explain. The most common, first, sign is a red ring at the site of the bite. This bulls-eye–looking red ring can enlarge to be about 20 centimeters, or almost 8 inches in diameter!! It can also turn into a rash and spread. So, you would think you couldn't miss it! The problem is that it only occurs in about two thirds of people who are infected. Some people develop a lesion that may be clear in the center resembling ringworm, or remain red and raised suggesting a skin infection. One third of infected people have no rash at all! Many people have a fever, headache, and muscle aches, like the garden-variety flu. Some people have no symptoms at all, in the beginning stage. This beginning stage of rash, no rash, or flulike symptoms can occur from 3 to 30 days after the tick bite!

The next stage of the infection occurs in weeks to months after the actual tick bite. Fifty percent of people develop symptoms of arthritis at this time. These recurring attacks of pain and swelling usually involve the knees and other large joints, lasting from days to a few weeks. Fever is sometimes common and usually high during this stage. Usually the attacks resolve completely, but they do tend to recur. Chronic arthritis is seen in about 10 percent of people infected.

Some more rare signs involve the nervous system. Meningitis and Bell's palsy (a drooping on one side of the face involving the eyelid and the lip—the nerve that controls these is infected) are the most common of these infrequent signs. Some people develop ataxia (dizziness) and vague fatigue. The heart can even be involved, in some dysfunction, from this infection.

Now that I have scared you, I will go into the treatment and prevention. As you might suspect, the diagnosis is not that easily made. That is why Juan's primary care provider wanted to see him as soon as possible. There are some laboratory tests, but even those have shown to be helpful in only a little over half of patients with early symptoms. Therefore, treatment is based upon clinical signs and a good history of exposure. Because treatment is beneficial in most cases, it is best if started early. The treatment of choice is usually amoxicillin, or erythromycin for children who have an allergy to penicillin. The length of treatment depends on the signs and symptoms and time from exposure. The primary care provider will discuss the treatment in more detail in each individual case.

Prevention is easy. Don't go where the ticks are! Now, I am only half kidding. However, if you do take the kids to the woods, have them wear long pants and long sleeves. The lighter the color, the better to see these tiny ticks! Use of tick repellents is recommended. You can spray it on the child's clothing. Repellents containing high concentrations of deet may cause neurologic symptoms and should be used cautiously and washed off when tick exposure ends. So please check the labels of these repellents and discuss their use with your parents. Your idea of checking each child after being outside is great. Your house is not in the woods, though you are in one of the known areas for deer ticks.

Q

Dear Nurse Libby,

Andy (18 months) has a strange looking rash on his leg, near his bottom. The doctor said that this is a yeast infection. Can you please explain what this is, and what the treatment might be? Is this contagious?

A

Dear Mrs. Kathy,

Rashes are difficult enough to describe over the phone. A written description is next to impossible. I'm glad there has been a diagnosis in this case. I assume by "his bottom" you are referring to his buttocks. I hope so, because yeast infections in this age group usually are related to the diaper area.

A yeast infection is an infection of the skin or mucous membranes (like the inside of the mouth), caused by a fungus. If the infection is on the skin, it is diagnosed usually by appearance. It appears as a beefy red area that includes the skin folds (as in a diaper rash). It can sometimes inch. The treatment is usually an antifungal topical cream or lotion. This medication is usually applied twice a day. Although, if the rash occurred inside the diaper area, the medication can be applied up to four times a day. The directions will be on the medication. There are various preparations on the market now to treat this infective rash.

As to it being contagious, usually yeast infections on the skin are not. There would have to be contact like sleeping in the same bed to increase the chance of spreading a topical fungus. The yeast fungus loves dark, moist areas. That is why the diaper area is a good place for them. If the rash had occurred in the mucous membranes, like the mouth, it could be contagious. I would not have anyone drink or eat after Andy. However, the yeast fungus is not usually airborne like the cold virus, so you don't have to plan for an epidemic. Hopefully, you use good hand-washing technique after diaper changes, after applying medications, and at meal times, to name a few instances. You could essentially have your hands in water more than they are out during the course of a day! Hopefully, you teach the children to not eat after each other, although that is sometimes hard to prevent! That is why good hand-washing technique for them, too, is so important.

Q

Dear Nurse Libby,

Kerrie has a strange rash that started on her face and spread to her body. She did not have a fever, so the school nurse allowed her to stay in school. Could this have been Fifth disease? If so, can you explain the disease and what I need to do? I heard that this could be a problem for pregnant women. Is this true?

A

Dear Mrs. Kathy,

It could have been Fifth disease (erythema infectiosum). How was she before the rash appeared? Let me explain! Erythema infectiosum is the fifth rash of childhood. It is caused by a virus that may, or may not, cause mild flulike symptoms prior to the onset of the rash. These symptoms include a low-grade fever, feeling tired, sore throat, and watery eyes. This is the time the person is contagious. This virus usually affects children between the ages of 5 and 15. It usually occurs in the spring or fall. By the time the rash appears, around 10 to 14 days after the onset, the contagious period is gone.

The rash itself is rather unique! The child initially looks like having been slapped on each cheek. The cheeks are warm, and the rash sometimes itches. The rash spreads to the forehead, chin, and around the ears. Two to three days later, the rash spreads to the arms, chest, and legs, sparing the palms of the hands and soles of the feet. As the rash fades, it does so from the center out. This produces a lacelike appearance to the skin. This fading rash may take several days to weeks to fade entirely. It may also reappear in response to local irritation (a warm bath, sunlight, and stress).

This is usually a mild, viral illness. The treatment is symptomatic. Treat any fever and body aches with appropriate medication. Allow the child to rest. If the child complains of itching, treat it.

As I stated, by the time the rash appears, the contagious period is over. Therefore, there is nothing anyone can do to prevent contact with a pregnant woman or anyone else. The virus that causes this rash can be dangerous to a pregnant woman. It can cause her to have a miscarriage. The only thing to be done is to test the woman for recent infection, if a serological test is available. If the test is positive, she should be followed for any fetal distress.

This virus can also have complications for the child, though rare. As with any virus, careful watching and treating symptoms are the best medicine.

Q

Dear Nurse Libby,

Recently Ricky (age three), had hand, foot, and mouth disease. Can you explain what this is and how he got it?

A

Dear Mrs. Kathy,

This syndrome does have a strange sound to the name. Hand, foot, and mouth disease is simply a virus. The virus has a strange name also, Coxsackie virus. This virus causes ulcerlike lesions in the mouth and a fine, red, raised rash on the palms of the hands and the soles of the feet. The child may or may not have a fever. The problem with this virus is that the ulcers in the mouth can be painful. When the child tries to eat or drink, it hurts too much and so the child may refuse to eat or drink. In severe cases, the child can become dehydrated. We treat the ulcers with a mixture of dyphenhydramine hydrochloride liquid and an antacid liquid. Depending on the age of the child, the mixture is either topically applied to the inside of the mouth, or the child is allowed to gargle with the solution and swallow it. This treatment is done four times a day—before meals and at bedtime. The amount of each liquid depends on the child's age and weight (as do most pediatric medications). For Ricky the dose would be 1 teaspoon of each mixed together. He, at age three, may or may not be able to swish it around in his mouth.

As I briefly stated, the problem with this virus is the possibility of the child dehydrating. It is important to get fluids into the child. As long as there are no other complications, such as vomiting and/or diarrhea, if you get the equivalent of 1 ounce of a liquid per hour into the child, the child most likely will not dehydrate. Don't worry about solid foods in the beginning stages of the illness if the child refuses to eat. As long as you keep the child hydrated, the child will most likely recover sooner with less complications.

This virus is contagious, as most viruses are. So obviously no one should share an infected child's food or drink. In your situation, if Ricky has a fever, he most likely won't be at the child care center during the initial contagious time of the disease.

The rash that appears on the palms of the hands and soles of the feet is a rash that you can feel. The fine red papules resolve on their own. Sometimes the palms and soles will peel as the infection resolves. Usually, there are no symptoms related to the rash and therefore, no treatment. I hope this information clears up the mystery of this strange illness.

Allergies

Q

Dear Nurse Libby,

One of the child care families has decided to get a kitten. The children are age three and five years of age, and I am not sure how they will handle a kitten. The father is allergic to cats. They already have a dog in the home, which they are not allergic to. What will the children be feeling if they are allergic to the kitten and they cannot keep it?

My suggestion was to visit with someone who has a cat to see how the children respond to the animal. Then they could determine whether they are allergic to cats or not. I also suggested that they visit a shelter or a pet store and watch how the children interact with the cat. This could determine if they are old enough to play with a kitten safely.

Could you give me a guide of how to determine when a child is ready for a pet, and how to pick the best pet for one's family?

I also have heard that children grow out of allergies if they are exposed to pets at an early age. Is there any truth to that?

A

Dear Mrs. Kathy,

This is an interesting question. Actually, I am more concerned about the father who has allergies to cats than I am about the children. Some studies have been done recently that have surprised the medical field. Children exposed to cats and dogs at an early age have been found to have fewer allergies than those children not exposed. Allergies are a result of the host being exposed to an allergen (some type of irritant) and the host reacting to this irritant. The reaction could be local—for example, itching or skin rash; or it could be systemic—for example, coughing or wheezing. The younger the child at time of exposure, the better the immune system can develop. So, it is advisable to have pets around with a child as early as you can. The real question is When are parents ready for pets? Parents must realize that they—not the child—will be the caregivers for the animal. Any new pet should be introduced slowly to the children. Because these children have a dog, they have had some exposure to animals. However, cats are a different animal. Your suggestions of visiting someone with a cat or visiting a shelter are good ones. The children can see how a cat looks, feels, and interacts with them. It would make a difference if the parents were getting a kitten or a full-grown cat. Kittens, like puppies, are young and have not yet developed their personality, so the adjustment to the new home would be easier.

There are no set guidelines for determining when to get a pet for one's family. Some people are animal lovers, and some are not. Again, I think the parents can determine first, whether they want an animal; second, when they want to have the animal; and third, what type of animal is good for them.

Many Web sites discuss these choices. Probably, the best site would be one that is written by a humane society. Articles on the subject of children, pets, and allergies also can be found on the Web. An excellent source of any health related issue is <http://www.webmd.com>.

Q

Dear Nurse Libby,

Cindy (age five) has been suffering terribly with allergies. She coughs, sneezes, and has watery eyes. Her doctor said that she is too young for allergy tests. He also prescribes only over-the-counter drugs, stating again that she is too young for anything stronger. This bothers me because my daughter (age eight), has been taking a prescription allergy medicine for years. Do you think Cindy should be on something stronger? Is there anything else I can do to help her with her allergies? Should I let her go outside to play?

A

Dear Mrs. Kathy,

First, every provider is different in his or her manner of prescribing. If the over-the-counter remedies help her, then leave her alone. However, I do not think they are helping her. If they were, her symptoms would not be as bad as you describe! Next question, do the symptoms bother her or you, or both? If she is not bothered by the symptoms, again, leave her alone.

If she is bothered by the symptoms, then you can recommend that her parents pursue treatment. You are correct that there are prescription medications that are age appropriate for a five-year-old. These medications are administered once a day, usually at bedtime. They seem to work quite well, as you have found out with your daughter. Back to Cindy, the only thing you can do for her is to suggest to her parents that they seek treatment with their primary care provider. Also remember that for any medication that you are to administer, you must have written permission from the parent. If it is a prescription drug, you also need a written order from the prescribing provider.

As for easing her symptoms, trying to keep her away from the allergen is a good thought. As long as the windows are open, keeping her inside is of little benefit. When you have the air conditioner on, keeping her inside will help her. She may prefer to suffer to be able to be with the other children. Let her be the guide; she will probably come inside for relief on and off during the day. One good thing about having allergies as a child is that sometimes symptoms are few as an adult.

Q

Dear Nurse Libby,

Robin (age three) got stung on the hand by a bee. Her hand began to swell at once. I applied ice and called her mother to come to get her. I was wondering if there is more I could have done. I have heard rumors about people going into shock over a bee sting. Should I be concerned?

A

Dear Mrs. Kathy,

People can go into shock over bee stings. It can be life threatening! Now that I have scared you, let me calm you down. There are different types of reactions to bee stings. Most people have what is called a local reaction. This is where only the part of the body that is actually stung reacts. For example, Robin's hand would be the only part of her body that became swollen. It might even be red and tender and itch. But, the swelling is localized to just her hand. If indeed that is what happened to Robin, applying ice is all that is necessary—that is, after you made sure the stinger was no longer in her hand.

The next type of reaction can be described as more of the same. The swollen, red, tender hand that itches now involves the arm. Again ice is the first line of defense. With this type of reaction, you could also give her an over-the-counter antihistamine. The swelling and itching are a result of the body releasing histamine to the site of trauma. Antihistamines help to counteract the reaction.

The most severe type of reaction is called a systemic reaction. This is exactly what it says. The whole body, the system, reacts to the bee sting. This reaction characteristically exhibits swelling, redness, itching, and tenderness of more than one part of the body. More important than this, though, is that usually this reaction involves difficulty in breathing. The breathing, sometimes referred to as stridor, is labored. This is the life-threatening reaction! The treatment of applying ice locally then giving an antihistamine is appropriate. This treatment, however, may not resolve the symptoms. This is the situation in which you call 911! While you are waiting for help, make sure the airway is always open. Use your CPR training. By the way everyone—parents and caregivers—should know CPR!!!! That is another subject. There are training sessions given locally everywhere. If you are not already, get certified!

A lot of people know they are allergic to bee stings, and to what extent. Those who suffer the severe reaction, and could possibly go into anaphylactic shock (the most severe reaction), usually have epinephrine on hand. This is called an epi-pen. This is an injection of adrenaline, and it requires a prescription. It is given as a needle under the skin. The person who has this type of reaction has been trained to use the injection at the first sign of a bee sting. If any of your children gets this reaction, I'm sure that the parent would inform you and have the proper medication on hand for you.

In your situation though, dealing with children, you may witness their first severe reaction! You will not have the epi-pen on hand. Therefore, I suggest you have ice and an appropriate antihistamine on hand. Maybe you should get permission from each parent to administer any type of antihistamine if a child is stung by a bee, as a first line of defense.

Q

Dear Nurse Libby,

When the children go outside to play, I am always concerned about sunburns. I usually apply a sunscreen that is recommended for children. I have noticed that some of the kids get a rash from the sunscreen with 45 SPF. Is this too strong for them? What do you recommend?

A

Dear Mrs. Kathy,

I say to most of my patients, "The sun is no longer our friend!" I'm really happy to read that you are using sunscreen on a regular basis! Some children may have sensitive skin and develop a rash to sunscreens. It really doesn't have to do with the SPF (sun protection factor). Let me explain. The sun protection factor (SPF) number on the label, tells you how long one can stay in the sun, without burning, after you have applied the sunscreen. The sunscreen will block the sun's rays (theoretically) for the time in minutes of the SPF number. Are you confused? Let me further explain. If you have a child who will normally burn after twenty minutes of sun exposure, using a sunscreen with an SPF of 15 gives 15 times the protection. The child can stay out in the sun for up to five hours and theoretically be protected from burning (20 minutes x 15 SPF = 300 minutes = 5 hours).

So you can see that using a sunscreen with a factor of 15 or higher should prevent both sunburn and tanning in a child six months and older when applied every couple of hours. You want to get a sunscreen that protects against both UVA and UVB rays. This protective factor will be listed on the label.

Back to your original question concerning sensitive skin. Any rash is probably the result of an ingredient in the sunscreen other than the SPF. To avoid possible skin reaction, use sunscreens that do not contain PABA. If that doesn't work, look for a product with the active ingredient titanium dioxide (a chemical-free block). This product is, as it states, free of any chemicals that can be allergy producing (like fragrances).

Another thought on allergies is for the infant under six months of age. These babies ideally should be kept out of the sun. Obviously, this is impossible to do. So, the next best thing is to protect them. Dress them in loose-woven clothing that covers the arms, shoulders, and legs. Let them wear a broad-brimmed hat. I love those on babies! Dressing them like this is the best sunscreen; however, if they are in the sun, use sunscreen on exposed skin areas. Use a sunscreen without fragrance and PABA definitely on these young babies. You can use a water-resistant sunscreen if the infant is getting into the water.

I thought I would add some guidelines for sunscreen use for the older baby and children. For sunscreen to work, it must be applied correctly. You should use sunscreen whenever the children are going outside into the sun. Apply it about a half hour prior to going out. This way a layer of protection can be formed. A thing that I see happen a lot is sunburn on the ears and feet! So don't forget lips, hands, ears, feet, behind the neck, and shoulders. Also, put the sunscreen under the edges of bathing suits and clothes. This will protect the child when clothes shift on them as they sometimes do (like shorts drooping on the hips, shoulder straps falling down, etc.). Sunscreen needs to be applied generously. Don't apply just a thin coat. Lather it on! If you are to be outside for the day, especially at the beach, reapply approximately every hour. There are waterproof sunscreens available that last up to approximately 80 minutes in the water. So these will have to be applied more often to those active water babies!

Every child needs extra protection from the sun. The American Academy of Dermatology recommends that all children use a sunscreen with an SPF of 15 or higher. Darker pigmented skin does have more protective melanin and tans more easily than it burns, but tanning is also a sign of sun damage. So you need to protect everyone. Remember, "The sun is no longer our friend!"

Shaken Baby Syndrome

Q

Dear Nurse Libby,

At a recent CPR class, I heard something that truly frightened me, and I hope that you can clear this up for me.

My instructor informed my class that a baby who is shaken does not die as soon as the action occurs, but several hours later. This means that a parent could be having a rough morning, lose his or her temper, shake the baby, put the child in a car seat and bring him or her to me, with the child appearing to be fine. I could place the child down for a nap, the baby's brain shifts while napping, and the child dies in my care. I, at this point, would be the prime suspect in the child's unfortunate death.

Is this true? Is this what occurs with shaken baby syndrome? Please explain what occurs when a child has experienced this type of injury, and if there are any signs to watch for.

A

Dear Mrs. Kathy,

This question is a very difficult one to answer. There is really no definite time period to help you. The CPR instructor was correct, in that it could take hours from the time of the actual incident to the time of death. This can be explained by describing the anatomy and physiology of what actually happens to the brain when a baby is shaken.

The baby is shaken. The neck and the head wobble back and forth. Inside, the brain too is shaken, it shifts back and forth, and a blood vessel ruptures. It is this bleeding that causes the death. If the rupture is a big one, death occurs quickly. If, however, the rupture is a tiny bleed, the hemorrhaging can take hours to be fatal. An autopsy could possibly locate the rupture site and evaluate the amount of bleeding. This could help determine an approximate time of the actual shaking.

There are some signs to look for that may help you. If an infant arrives in the morning either too drowsy or too irritable, either could be a subtle sign of head trauma. If the infant's pupils are unequal, or if there is blood or a clear discharge from the ear or nose of an otherwise healthy infant, question the parent. Another obvious sign is if the infant or toddler who can normally sit, stand, and/or walk is suddenly unsteady with either sitting, standing, or walking. Another obvious sign would be if the infant has a seizure. Of course, that would be an emergency in a child care center!

What I am trying to say is that there are no definite, clear-cut guidelines for you. All you can do is be alert to any change(s) in the normal behavior of the infant.

Staring Spells

Q

Dear Nurse Libby,

Marla (age four) has a bad habit of staring at me, without answering, when I ask her a question. I can ask her what she would like for breakfast, and she will stand there and stare at me. I have relayed my concern to her mother, and she comments that Marla's pre-K teacher has expressed the same concern. I asked her mother if she had considered having her tested to check whether Marla has a learning disability. Her mother just replies, "I guess she's just slow!" When Marla stands and stares at me, should I continue to ask the question or just walk away? Should I be concerned that she may have a disability, and, if so, how do I get the mother involved?

A

Dear Mrs. Kathy,

The symptoms you describe for Marla concern me. You are describing staring spells. This is not a bad habit, nor is it a learning disability. It is usually a sign of a type of seizure disorder—petit mal. This illness can be treated with medication, allowing Marla a normal life. This seizure disorder is the mildest form of seizures and, once treated, normally does not interfere with a child's ability to participate in all childhood activities.

She deserves an evaluation. Encourage the mother to take Marla to her primary care provider. The primary care provider will do a complete history and physical examination. The mother needs to share your and the pre-K teacher's evaluation of Marla with the primary care provider. The evaluation would include two noninvasive diagnostic tests—a CT scan and an EEG—to determine a seizure disorder. Keep me posted on Marla.

Q

Dear Nurse Libby,

Marla is now five years old and is a very sweet child. She still stares at me and will not answer questions. She has been put in a special group at school, and I can only hope that she will receive any necessary help she may need.

A

Dear Mrs. Kathy,

Hopefully the school can give Marla the help she needs. I still think she deserves a neurological workup.

Orthopedic Issues

Q

Dear Nurse Libby,

Latoya (age six) can bend her fingers in several unusual positions. She said that she is double-jointed. What exactly is that? Is it something that a person outgrows? Is it harmful to the joints?

A

Dear Mrs. Kathy,

Double-jointed is a term we use to describe joints that have more mobility than what is considered normal range of motion. To further explain hypermobility of joints, as it is sometimes referred to, I will have to go into a little bit of the anatomy and physiology of joints. Ligaments are a type of tissue that connect bone to bone and provide joint stability. A tendon is a type of tissue that connects bone to muscle and provides joint mobility. Hypermobility of joints occurs when this connective tissue is more loose than normal. The ability to pop joints in and out, as Latoya can do, is a result of this laxity in the joints. Allowing the child to flex and exercise the joint to its full range of motion is okay and doesn't usually cause any harm.

In most cases, children will outgrow this laxity. The connective tissue tightens as the child gets older. The condition does not contribute to arthritis any more frequently than in a child who never experiences this phenomenon. It occurs in only about 5 percent of the population.

Several disorders, however, cause joint instability, not just joint hypermobility. These disorders have other joint and bone symptoms along with the hypermobility. You would probably already know the child's diagnosis.

The other interesting occurring syndrome that is worth mentioning is hypermobility syndrome. This is now recognized as a frequent cause of joint pain. This syndrome is caused by the ligaments of a joint becoming loose (laxity) as a result of increased physical activity. Children are now participating in a wide range of sports that are physically demanding. The typical scenario is that a child complains of joint pain and sometimes swelling after a sports activity. The symptoms usually last only a few days after the exertion. Along with joint pain and swelling is seen joint laxity. This is usually seen as hyperextension of a joint like the elbow, knee, or even a finger or thumb. The treatment consists of proper conditioning of the joint by strengthening muscles around the joint, to compensate for the loose ligaments. The condition usually resolves if the child is consistent with the conditioning program.

So if Latoya can bend her fingers in several unusual positions and experiences no pain, let her.

Q

Dear Nurse Libby,

I have been noticing recently that Marla's (age five) feet turn inward. I guess they have always been like that, but the other day she was wearing dress shoes and it was quite obvious. I spoke to her mother about it, and she stated that when she was a baby she had to wear shoes with a bar in the middle of them to try to straighten her legs. She said that her doctor feels that her legs will straighten the rest of the way in time. They look like they are getting worse. Does this sound normal to you or should her mother seek a second opinion?

A

Dear Mrs. Kathy,

"Toeing-in," as it is usually referred to, is a normal developmental variant. When this occurs in infancy, it is usually caused by the lower leg (between the knee and ankle) turning in. This internal rotation usually corrects itself by 16 to 18 months of age. If it still persists at this age, sometimes a splint is worn at night to externally rotate (turn out) the legs. This is probably the shoes with the bar that Marla's mother was referring to.

Toeing-in after the age of 2 to 3 years actually involves the femur, the large bone in the top of the leg. The femur is turned toward the body, so naturally the feet turn inward. This inward rotation gradually decreases around 8 years of age. It may take up to age 16 for the rotation to reach normal adult alignment.

Some orthopedic specialists treat this condition with braces and special shoes that turn the feet outward. Studies have been done, though, comparing this treatment with just leaving them alone, and have found no real difference in the time frame to reach normal alignment. Certain activities such as ballet, skating, and bicycle riding have shown slight improvement. The reason for this is simple if you think about it. Look at the shape of a ballet shoe and a skate. They both force the foot to be almost straight, if not make the foot turn outward. The bicycle also keeps the femur straight. So as growth occurs, the bone will have a better chance of growing straight, not inward.

As long as Marla has been evaluated, she is probably just fine. Let her ride a bike, skate, and dance on her toes as much as she wants. However, in Marla's case in particular, if she has not been evaluated for the staring spells (discussed on page 24), you will need to monitor her activities more closely. I advise you to have her wear a helmet when bike riding and skating, as all children should.

Q

Dear Nurse Libby,

My daughter (age eight) is constantly complaining that she has twisted her ankle. She has been to the school nurse several times, and will come home with her ankle wrapped up. I have never noticed any swelling or bruising. I do notice that she trips a lot. Her doctor has said not to worry; she just has weak ankles. What do you think?

A

Dear Mrs. Kathy,

The doctor may be right. I need more information, though. You say she has no swelling or discoloration. This is a good thing. Does the wrapping—an ace bandage, I assume—make it feel better? If so, she may indeed have weak ankles. Her tripping a lot concerns me. Because she did go to the doctor, I'm assuming that he did an evaluation. This evaluation should normally include a complete examination of her legs, including her hips and her feet. Tripping can be a sign of either in-toeing (metatarsus adductus), or legs turning in (internal tibial torsion). The latter can involve hip rotation.

The evaluation should also include how she walks, leg lengths, and the range of motion of her hips. Sometimes radiographic examinations (X rays) are necessary, especially of the hip, to make sure there is no slip of the hip bone.

If this evaluation is normal, she may indeed have weak ankles, a condition she should outgrow. There are some strengthening exercises she can do. She could also benefit from shoes that provide extra support for her ankles. High-top tennis shoes are the most common. Just make sure that whatever shoes she does wear are form fitting. Stay away from sandals that have no supportive strap. Definitely, no shoes with a heel! Actually, the best way to strengthen weak ankles is to walk in bare feet a lot!

Urinary Tract Infections

Q

Dear Nurse Libby,

I recently noticed that Marla (age five) was constantly running to the bathroom. I asked her if she was all right, and she said that she felt pain when she urinated. I called her mother and told her that I was suspicious that Marla may have a bladder infection. She took her to her health care provider and my guess was right! What could have caused this infection? Is there anything that I can do to prevent it from happening again?

A

Dear Mrs. Kathy,

What could have caused this infection, indeed! Let me explain my superlative! Urinary tract infections in children seem to be a problem for some children, whereas others may never experience a one. The type of urinary tract infection that you explained—a bladder, or lower urinary tract—is the most common and has an excellent prognosis. It is usually caused by poor personal hygiene and most often affects young girls around Marla's age or younger. These girls usually do not wipe themselves correctly. The correct method is to wipe from front to back, and not back and forth. Other common causes are pinworms, sexual abuse or activity (in the older female child), humidity, and bubble baths. Let me explain these. Pinworms are a rectal infection that can spread to the urethra (the opening through which the child urinates). Sexual abuse or activity can cause irritation and inflammation to the urethra and allow bacteria to enter. Obviously, if sexual abuse is suspected, it must be reported! By humidity, I mean the genital area being surrounded by moisture. For instance, if a child wears a bathing suit all day, or tights, or heavy jeans, the genital area is constantly moist. This moisture allows for bacteria to grow and possibly enter the urethra, resulting in a bladder infection. Though not that simple, the result is the same! Bubble bath is a source of many bladder infections. The actual bubble soap affects some children by causing an inflammation, which sets the wheels in motion for the bladder infection.

There are some less common reasons for these infections. Some children are sensitive to nylon or silk panties. These panties do not allow the genital area to dry properly, thus the inflammation scenario is set up. This results in a bladder infection. These children should wear all cotton underwear. Some children, who may be predisposed to diabetes, may get a bladder infection if they drink a lot of liquids high in sugar, like soda or powdered drinks. These children usually experience more than one infection.

Any child who experiences symptoms similar to Marla's or abdominal pain, vomiting, strong-smelling urine, the urge to go frequently, or bedwetting (in an otherwise dry child) should be evaluated for a urinary tract infection. Little girls are allowed two infections, if they appear to be a simple lower tract infection, before a workup is done. Little boys, for anatomical reasons, are only allowed one infection before a workup is done. This workup involves tests to try and find a reason for the infections. These reasons usually involve anatomical abnormalities, most of which can be treated. So it is very important for the child to be followed through the evaluation process, even if the child seems to be free of symptoms.

Maybe you can now answer the second part of your question yourself! You can monitor the children's wiping patterns more closely. If you teach the children how to wipe and use good hand-washing techniques, you could hopefully prevent a lot of these infections. You can look for signs of pinworms, the cardinal sign of which is rectal itching—the child who is constantly scratching his rectum! You can monitor the clothing the children wear. Especially in the summer, don't allow the children to live in their bathing suits. You can increase water in their diet, replacing sweetened beverages. If you are diligent in these things, you are doing all you can do to help the children.

Medications

Q

Dear Nurse Libby,

One of my parents has asked me to give her daughter (age three) a prescription cough medicine that was given to her last year. I was not comfortable giving her this medicine because the child had not been seen by the health care provider for the cough. Also I would assume that the dose should be different. Was I right to refuse to give this medicine?

A

Dear Mrs. Kathy,

Yes, you were right to refuse to give her the medication. A medication that was given to a child a year ago may have expired. The three-year-old has probably gained weight in the past year also. Prescription medication dosing, especially for children, is based on weight and age. Prescription medications are given for specific illnesses, which need to be diagnosed prior to dispensing the medications.

If the mother had talked with the primary care provider, and had agreed that the medication was warranted, and agreed on a proper dose for the child, and if the medication had not expired, you could have been safe in giving her the medication. Usually, prescription cough preparations are given for children with chronic conditions such as asthma and seasonal allergies. However, the type of cough is different for each of these conditions. Some children have to take medication for these illnesses on a regular basis, whereas others need the medication only when symptoms occur episodically. Hopefully, you would know if any child in your care has a chronic condition requiring medication, and you would have that medication on hand with specific instructions.

The other types of cough medication that require a prescription are usually given to a child who may have bronchitis or pneumonia. These children need an evaluation by their primary care provider prior to administration of the medication. So, for all these reasons, you were correct to refuse to give the medication. If the child's cough persisted, hopefully the mother contacted her primary care provider for advice or a visit. Remember to always follow the guidelines provided by your local state licensing agency concerning dispensing prescription and over-the-counter medications.

Vision

Q

Dear Nurse Libby,

I have noticed that kids, starting at about two years old, love to sit very close to the television set when it is on—so close, in fact, that usually a fight will start over who is going to sit the closest! Have you ever tried to sit that close to the TV? I have, and it appeared to me to be a big blob of colored dots, and certainly not comfy on the neck. So what gives? Why do children sit so close to the TV? Is it truly bad for their eyesight?

A

Dear Mrs. Kathy,

Children are born farsighted (hyperopia). That is why newborns will focus and follow when the object is held about twelve inches away from them. The child's vision progresses to the normal 20/20 around two to three years of age. This change is a progressive one. So, the child may actually be nearsighted and need to sit close to the TV at this early age. By the time they are two to three years old, as in the group you are describing, they should be able to see the TV from a normal distance. I would encourage you to have them sit back a normal distance.

I think that what is going on with them wanting to sit so close to the TV is a peer thing! What I mean is that for two-year-olds the activity on TV is very stimulating. They get excited. Most two-year-olds think that the world centers on them. So each of them wants to be first, or in front! You, as a child care provider, have more than one two-year-old! They start competing with each other. So you end up having them competing to be closest to the TV. Have them sit back. The overstimulation could weaken their vision.

Burns

Q

Dear Nurse Libby,

One of the child care children grabbed an iron while at home. When the mother brought the child to me, she stated that she had put butter on the burn. Is this treatment something that you would advise? I have always heard to run cold water over a burn and then keep it clean and dry. Please tell me your treatment method.

A

Dear Mrs. Kathy,

The first step in treating a burn is to cool it down. The best way to do that is with a cold compress, usually ice. Running cold water on the burn is good also. The pressure from the water may cause more pain, though. The child may need something for pain. In your situation, a dose of acetaminophen, according to the child's age, is appropriate. Most burns are superficial. What I mean is that the area is red, dry, and painful. That is the reason for the treatment I described. If a burn starts to blister, clean it and cover it with an antibacterial ointment and dressing. This keeps infection from starting, because the skin is broken and infection can get to the deeper layers of the skin.

A child with deep and painful blisters should be seen by a healthcare provider. Blisters often need to be debrided to heal with minimal infection and scarring. Any burn on the face, hand, feet, or genital area is considered major and needs to be evaluated as soon as possible.

The other worry for you while accepting children with a fresh burn is whether or not the burn is a symptom of abuse. Being around the families and children all the time, I'm sure that you have a feel for what the family life is like. I'm afraid, though, that sometimes even the best of us can be fooled. I would suggest that if more than one burn occurs to a child, you should call the state and see what your choices are. It is a hard thing to face, but abuse occurs everywhere.

Now, back to the butter. The use of butter to treat a burn is an old remedy. The only reason to put butter on a burn is because butter usually is cold. The only problem is that it may cause an infection in a burn that has open blisters. So now that we have refrigeration and available ice, use cold compresses!

Splinters

Q

Dear Nurse Libby,

Today we went to the boardwalk in the neighborhood and took a walk. Ricky (age four), fell and got a splinter in his hand. I could see that the splinter was at the tip of the skin, so I removed it with a pair of tweezers. Then I cleaned the wound and applied a bandage. Would it have been better to leave the splinter alone and let it come out on its own?

A

Dear Mrs. Kathy,

A splinter is a foreign body to our skin. If it stays in, the site could become infected. This infection would be the body's way of trying (unsuccessfully) to rid itself of the foreign body. The way you proceeded to remove the splinter was the correct first-aid procedure. The only reason I can think of to let a splinter come out on its own would be if the splinter was so superficial that it was on its way out already. Even then, I would advise to help it finish the job!

Growing Pains

Q

Dear Nurse Libby,

Andy (age eighteen months) screamed and cried all day today. I tried every thing to help him. Finally I took his pants off to check his temperature, and the crying stopped. I noticed that he had a mark around his stomach from the band on his pants. I checked the rest of his body and there were no other marks or rashes. I guess the pants were too tight and he was miserable. Lucky for me, I require all parents to bring a change of clothes for their children. Just something to think about when you have parents calling you with a crying child!

A

Dear Mrs. Kathy,

Thank you! That is a very easy remedy for a crying toddler! It happens more often than one would think. Children experience their growth spurts at various intervals. A green light does not come on, saying that the child is growing. The toddler is such a picky eater that even an increase in his appetite can go unnoticed! He is usually not verbal enough at this age to tell anyone that he is hungrier than usual. Andy did the only thing he could do to explain his discomfort. He cried.

However, if the crying had persisted, Andy would have needed to be seen by his primary care provider. The toddler's only way of communicating pain is to cry persistently! This is especially true if the child has no other physical symptoms, such as a fever, vomiting, or diarrhea.

Q

Dear Nurse Libby,

Ricky (age five) has been complaining of leg pains, usually after we have been to the playground and back. I told his mother about this, and she stated that he has been waking up during the night, crying because his legs hurt! What could this be? What should we do?

A

Dear Mrs. Kathy,

This is a very common complaint of childhood. It usually has a very simple explanation—growing pains! Yes, believe it or not, there is such a thing! Think about it. Our muscles, bones, and joints are growing during childhood growth spurts. The problem is that they don't all grow at the same rate at the same time. This inequality of growth can cause at least one to be stretched or strained. This results in the pain. It is usually felt in the legs of children, the long bones.

However, if the child complains of painful joints, and/or if there is swelling and/or redness, the child needs to be seen by the primary care provider. Some causes of these symptoms are juvenile arthritis or a bacterial or viral infection of the joint. These are serious illnesses and need to be treated as soon as possible.

Ricky's source of pain needs to be defined. If indeed, his pain is along the long bone with no other symptoms, the treatment is easy. Give him ibuprofen to treat the inflamed area that is being stretched or strained at the time of growth. Of course, you would discuss this treatment with his parents and get their approval before giving him anything.

Chapter 2

LETTERS ON DEVELOPMENT

Sucking Urge

Q

Dear Nurse Libby,

I have been watching Andy since he was two weeks old, and ever since he was born he always sucked on blankets. He never showed interest in a thumb or a pacifier. He is now two years old and he still sucks on his blanket. He is constantly sticking toys in his mouth as well. Is this okay for him to continue? I only allow the blankets at naptime.

A

Dear Mrs. Kathy,

What you are describing here is a normal phenomenon for all babies—the sucking urge! All infants are born with the sucking reflex. For obvious reasons, it is necessary for survival. If the infant does not have a strong sucking reflex, he or she will not be able to drink either formula or breast milk easily. This could result in low weight gain and developmental delay. However, that is another issue.

What Andy is displaying is the continuing of the sucking urge. In some babies, this reflex is very strong and continues into toddlerhood (age one to three years). Some babies, Andy being one of them, need to suck a lot. That is why a lot of providers, myself included, recommend a pacifier for all infants. The infant will let the parent know how often they need the pacifier. Infants with a strong sucking urge who are not given a pacifier will find something else to suck on! They will not stop sucking just because they do not have a nipple handy. Fingers, thumbs, and blankets are the most common things the infant finds to suck. Once the habit is started, they will prefer the chosen object to suck until the urge is gone. The urge usually weakens and is gone by the time the child is four or five years old.

Parents can help in the weaning of the "pacifier" (whatever it is). Infants should be allowed to suck as often as they want. When the infant is over one year of age, the pacifier should be given at bedtimes and times when the toddler is irritable (those whining times). Sucking helps to calm the toddler and allows toddlers to learn how to go to sleep and to "settle their nerves." By the age of two to three years the toddler learns to "settle nerves" in other ways. They are old enough for time-out. Therefore, the pacifier should not be used during whining times at this age. It can still be used to help a restless toddler learn to settle down for sleep. Usually, if weaned in this fashion, most toddlers will give up the pacifier on their own. The sucking urge will fade away, and the toddler will no longer need the pacifier.

This weaning process works best with the traditional pacifier. If the infant develops the habit of using a thumb or finger, the habit will last longer. The body part cannot be weaned away by an adult! Concerns with thumb sucking are skin infections and abnormal tooth development. The thumb and finger can actually push the teeth out of proper alignment. This could then lead to the need for braces. The blanket seems to be more socially accepted by adults, so it too will take longer to wean from the child. Other concerns arise with the use of blankets. The child could rip off a piece of the blanket and swallow it. The traditional pacifier is made to allow proper teeth development. It is also quite safe with no detachable parts.

Fearless Toddlerhood

Q

Dear Nurse Libby,

While I was assisting another child, Samantha (a little over one year old) climbed on top of my picnic table and was ready to jump before I stopped her. At home she put a chair on a table and climbed on the table and fell off the chair. She cried and received a large lump on the head. As soon as no one was looking, she did it again.

Are there any ways that you know to teach her the danger in what she is doing?

A

Dear Mrs. Kathy,

I'm afraid not! Let me explain. Samantha is a little over one year of age. Remember, this is the age of exploration! One- to two-year-old toddlers have no fear. They are out there exploring their world, not thinking things like, "This is high and I could fall and hurt myself!" Some toddlers are more "explorative" than others. They have literally no impulse control. These are the toddlers who climb everything that is not flat! They will also put most anything in their mouth. They will bite, pull hair, and/or pinch most any living thing also!

They are quick! A study was done in the 1960s about their activity level. College football players, supposedly in the peak of physical ability, could not keep up with active toddlers.

They also are just learning structure and control. They are learning as much as they can. They may not remember tomorrow what you told them yesterday.

All you can really do at this age is to protect Samantha from hurting herself and others. You can do this by distracting her from the negative behavior and redirecting her to a behavior that is positive and safe.

Q

Dear Nurse Libby,

Andy (age one) has finally started to walk. I do not allow him near the steps, and I am required by the child care administration to place a gate at the steps. His parents want him exposed to the steps so that he can learn how to climb them. What is your advice on children and steps?

A

Dear Mrs. Kathy,

At Andy's age, you are correct to put up a gate for steps. As you said, he has finally started to walk, at the age of one year old. I'm almost sure that his balance is not the best yet. He probably runs and falls sometimes on level ground. A one-year-old's coordination is still progressing. Steps take coordination to master correctly. Usually, by age two, toddlers master steps by walking up and down successfully.

You would be taking a chance that he would go to the steps, lose his balance, fall, and really hurt himself. A toddler's bones are soft and break easily! If his parents want to expose him to steps, you could suggest climbing toys or slides. If your state regulations allow, you could offer these type of climbing toys also. These toys help to develop the coordination necessary to master stair climbing. So follow your state rules and keep the gate up.

Speech Delay

Q

Dear Nurse Libby,

Robin, who is almost two years old, is still not speaking. When she wants something, she groans and points. I will take the object that she is pointing at and say what it is to her in hopes that she will repeat it. Instead she just grunts and points. She does say "mama" and "dada," and sometimes she will try to repeat what I say. However, she does not come close to repeating it. She can hum songs from start to finish, so I know she can hear. Is this something to be concerned about?

Dear Nurse Libby,

I have recently noticed Robin (almost two years) has been trying to chew on a wicker rocking chair.

A

Dear Mrs. Kathy,

I have taken the liberty to combine the two questions on Robin. They may or may not be related. I have some questions for you, though. First, concerning her speech: Does she understand what is said to her? Her comprehension level is her receptive speech. Receptive, or understanding everything said to her, developmentally can occur before verbal speech. So, if she can understand most things said to her, follow commands like "Pick that toy up and put it here," her verbal speech should follow. You state that she says "mama" and "dada." Hopefully, she is saying these words, just denoting her mother and father. If she says "mama" and "dada" to everyone, that is a developmental delay and demands notice.

Eating the wicker chair at almost two years of age is also a developmental delay. A lot of one-year-old toddlers still chew almost anything. By the age of two, this habit is disappearing, as most of the primary teeth have erupted.

These two developmental delays are something to be concerned about. Robin deserves an evaluation. More questions: Are her parents remodeling an old house? Has her lead level been checked? It should be checked routinely at one year of age and repeated at two years of age. An elevated lead level could cause both of the symptoms you have described. Her primary care provider who will most likely do at least a lead level and a hearing test on Robin should see her.

If the tests are within normal limits and her receptive language is normal, she is just lagging behind a little with speech. Some children understand everything and do not speak till they "get it right"! Their beginning speech is complete sentences! The chair eating could then be a result of teething. She may be having a hard time cutting her two-year molars and/or be lagging behind in teething all together. Remember, also, that teething is very individual and NOT a sign of developmental delay.

Q

Dear Nurse Libby,

Nick (age 2½ years) will not say a word. He will sometimes say "dada" or "nana" but not in relation to a person. I feel that he is delayed in his speech. When he wants something, he points and grunts or screams. I will try to get him to say the word before I give him the object. This however leads to great frustration for him.

Should I suggest that his parents have him tested for developmental delays, or am I rushing things?

I can get him to follow instructions to clean up, come here, or not to touch something. He is a very pleasant little boy, whose only form of communication is to grunt and point.

A

Dear Mrs. Kathy,

Yes, I think you should suggest to his parents to have Nick tested for speech delay. At the age of two years and four months, he should have at least 10 words. Some toddlers, at the age of two can speak in complex sentences. As you can see, there is a wide range of normal. However, definitely by Nick's age, he should be saying "dada" or "nana" to a particular person. Usually, by two years this developmental milestone is met.

The good thing I can see for Nick is his receptive language. The fact that he can follow instructions shows that he can understand what is said to him. Because he understands and follows commands, his hearing is most likely normal. You did not suggest in your question that you were concerned about that. Nick still deserves a complete workup. The speech and language evaluation can, in some states, be obtained from the speech therapist at the elementary school in the district where he lives. He should also be seen by his primary care provider for a complete physical examination to rule out any medical reasons for his delay. A hearing test should also be performed.

Depending on the outcome of these evaluations, Nick may be seen by a pediatric developmental psychologist, or pediatric neurologist, or other specialists as needed. If speech therapy is necessary, it can sometimes be done by the speech pathologist at the school. Sometimes, speech therapy will take place over three to four years.

As I already stated, the good thing I can see for Nick, is his receptive language. I have seen some children who understand everything that is said to them. They just don't say too many words until they can speak in sentences. If, however, Nick, is over the age of three and is still grunting and pointing, I would be even more concerned.

Diaper Changing Rituals

Q

Dear Nurse Libby,

As part of my diaper-changing ritual I apply baby skin care lotion all over the children: face, tummy, arms, legs, and back. I find that the children love the feeling of the lotion, and I love spending a little special time pampering them. One of my moms stated that her 18-month-old got a pimple on his leg, and she feels that the baby lotion is what caused it. I have been using lotion on him since he was two weeks old. I would hate to stop using the lotion because I feel that it is good both mentally and physically for the children. Do you think the lotion could have caused the pimple? Do you have suggestions on lotions I should use and how often I should use them?

A

Dear Mrs. Kathy,

Yes, I am afraid to tell you, the lotion could have caused his pimple. Babies usually have very soft skin; they require no added lotion. I can understand and appreciate you wanting to make diaper changing a pleasant time, especially with the toddler (but that is another topic altogether).

It is recommended that no lotion or baby oil be used on the face of an infant or child and used only on dry areas of other parts of the body, excluding the diaper area. They are born with naturally moist skin. Older generations used to use baby oils and lotions, possibly due to the fact that they had harsh soaps, which dried the skin. The soaps we have now are quite mild. Adding lotion can cause baby acne, clogged pore—thus the pimple. This reaction can occur on other parts of the body.

The exception to the rule is, however, a baby born with the skin condition eczema. These babies have dry, sometimes scaling skin. They require globs of nonscented moisturizing lotion applied three or four times a day. Sometimes a medicated cream is prescribed. It should be applied as directed by the health care provider.

Back to the diaper area—this is an area we want to keep dry. Lotions would only add moisture there as well. Diaper care products that contain zinc oxide are the best. This ingredient provides a shield to protect the skin from the irritants in the urine and stool. If you have ever tried to remove zinc oxide, it is not easily washed off even with soap and water. You must first remove it with a lubricant such as baby lotion, or oil. Then wash the lubricant off, pat the skin dry, and reapply the zinc oxide.

I'm sure you can make diaper changing a fun ritual in another way. Let me know what you come up with.

Dear Mrs. Kathy,

While we are discussing diaper changing, I want to discuss the diaper changing of the toddler. This refers to the child between the ages of one and three years old. They are now able to walk (that is why they are called the toddler—they toddler around). Most of the time they are in fast mode, also. So, to tackle the job of changing a toddler is high risk! You must try to stay two steps ahead of their every move! They wiggle and turn so quickly, they can be at high risk themselves, for falls off of changing tables.

I suggest that you try to distract them! Give them something to do while being changed. Have them participate in the act. Give them a rattle, book, or toy to play with. Allow them to hold the new diaper, but watch out for holes in the new diaper. Everything goes into the mouths of these toddlers, also! Have pictures or mobiles around for the baby to look at. Sing a song or funny limerick. They are learning to talk now and like to hear new and different sounds. Changing a toddler is like changing a moving target. So, be safe while changing them and have fun with your toddler!

Toilet Training

Q

Dear Nurse Libby,

The twin's (age 2½ years) mom and I have started to potty train the girls. They certainly have the interest to go, but the problem is that they have to go every 15 minutes. Could this mean that they are not ready? They do make it through the night without wetting!

A

Dear Mrs. Kathy,

If they are able to make it through the night and stay dry and are not having a lot of accidents during the day, they are ready. What is most likely happening is that they are impressed with themselves for being able to produce in the potty! They are, also, probably competing with each other. Are you praising them and rewarding them for using the potty and not having accidents? This is the normal process in potty training children. We reward them for succeeding. Being twins, they see each other being rewarded; they know how to obtain the reward, so they go more often. The other thing that happens at this age is that most two- to three-year-olds drink fluids all the time! Therefore, they have to go more frequently. As long as they are successful, not having a lot of accidents, they are ready. Let them go as often as they wish. The novelty will wear off and they will go at normal intervals. It will happen sooner if you treat what they are doing in our "matter-of-fact" manner. This too shall pass! It's got to be better than changing two sets of diapers!

Q

Dear Nurse Libby,

The twins will be three years old in two weeks and are doing very well with potty training. At naptime I have been putting them both in a pull-up. Do you think that this is confusing to them? Should I let them sleep in their big girl pants?

A

Dear Mrs. Kathy,

This is a topic where there is a lot of confusion. Toilet training seems to concern some parents and caregivers more than others. It is a stage of development, just like walking and talking. The toddler has to be at the right development for the process to occur. First, the toddler (one- to three-year-old) has to be able to talk in small sentences to be able to communicate the need to toilet. Second, the toddler must have the muscle control to be able to hold the toileting process until he or she is at the toilet. Third, and most important, the toddler must have the interest or desire to use the toilet instead of diapers.

As far as the pull-ups go, when you are toilet training a child, it is confusing to put them in diapers sometimes and panties sometimes. They then not only have to have the three skills just mentioned here, but they have to think about what they are wearing also! Pull-ups were invented to be worn in the in-between stage. If the girls are not having accidents at night, they should be fine at naptime. Remember to have the children use the bathroom before they lay down for a nap.

Q

Dear Nurse Libby,

I am happy to report that Jenny and Penny have successfully completed potty training. It was rough in the beginning because we were constantly running to the bathroom. It is definitely better than changing two sets of diapers all the time!

A

Dear Mrs. Kathy,

I am so glad that things have worked out with the twins and their toilet training. We parents and caregivers sometimes stress out over some things that are a part of normal growth and development. Toilet training is definitely one of these things.

Here are some actual stories on toilet training to prove that it is just another developmental stage. Girls usually are toilet trained between 18 months and 2 years. Boys are usually trained between 2 and 2½ years.

My oldest son was 2½ years old when he was toilet trained. I tried at 18 months—no luck; at two years—no luck. Then around 2½ years of age, we were riding in the car on a day trip. I had run out of diapers (real diapers too)! He was going to take a nap in the car. I had just changed him, using my last diaper. I looked around and found in the car a mayonnaise jar! (I was saving them for my mother-in-law who used them for canning foods.) I showed it to him and said, "When you wake up, if you don't wet your diaper, you can pee-pee in this jar." He said okay and went to sleep. I told his dad we might as well head for home, as our son will most likely be wet when he awakes. Well, he woke up, asked for the jar and used it! He was so proud of himself. We had to use a jar for a short period of time. We had to take the jar in the bathroom. We slowly replaced the jar with the toilet. He never wore a diaper after that day. We also kept a jar in the car for emergencies for a long time. I realize this technique is unique for boys only.

His brother was 20 months old when he was toilet trained. The reason I remember is that he announced that morning that he wanted to wear BBPs (big boy pants). I had tried him at 18 months and at 2 years with similar results as his brother. It was summertime, and I had a teenage baby-sitter for them on a part-time basis. I was getting ready to leave for work one morning, the baby-sitter had arrived, and my son made his request. I looked at her and asked if she felt comfortable with his request. She said fine, and off came the diaper, on went the BBPs. He has never worn a diaper since.

My cousin has two adorable little girls a year apart. The oldest, at three, just became toilet trained. Sometimes, when children are close together, the older one does not want to grow up, thinking she has been replaced by the younger one. Her cousins who are four were with her recently. They have been trained for over a year and thought she wore big girl panties also. They were discussing this and were shocked to find out she was still wearing diapers. They informed her that she should be wearing big girl panties like they do. Her mother reports that on the very next day, her oldest daughter awoke and asked for big girl pants. She has been toilet trained ever since. Her younger sister is even thinking about it.

What these examples show is that this process is the first stage of independence. You, of course, have to introduce the process to them, usually at 18 months. You take them to the bathroom with you, let them sit on potty chairs, throw water in the toilet, flush the toilet, wear the BBPs, and so on. The actual training occurs when they have the muscle control, are verbally able to tell someone, and have the desire and interest. Also there are many great books available on potty training for children and adults to read.

Q

Dear Nurse Libby,

Ricky (age 3½) is finally potty trained, and now that he is not wearing a diaper he constantly is playing with his penis. Is this normal? How should I handle this situation?

A

Dear Mrs. Kathy,

Ricky is at the right age to be noticing his body parts. The three- to five-year-old realizes the differences between boys and girls. This is the age of masturbation. It is quite normal. Some children do it more often than others. Some don't even realize they are doing it.

If Ricky does it in a private place, just ignore him. I'm sure it is hard to find a private place at a child care center, though. You should have a talk with him, with his parent's permission and/or their presence. You discuss it with him, at his level of understanding. The points to cover are that his body parts are private and that he touches them only in private. You will remind him with a mutual signal when he is doing it in front of the other children. You can include that no one else is to touch him in that manner also.

This may be a delicate issue for everyone. However, in this day and time, it is highly important.

Q

Dear Nurse Libby,

Is it normal for a five-year-old child be so interested in an activity that he would wet his pants and remain sitting there until the other children started making fun of him? I was concerned that he might have a bladder infection, so I asked him why he wet himself. He told me that he could not hold it until he was finished with the activity. I should also point out that recently, when using the potty, he has been missing and wetting the floor! I have considered putting a target on the bottom of the toilet.

A

Dear Mrs. Kathy,

On the subject of the five-year-old boy who is wetting his pants and the bathroom floor, there are reasons and answers! Putting a target on the bottom of the toilet is a possible solution for that problem, though.

Most children at this age have occasional accidents. They do not want to take time away from play, or other interests, to go to the bathroom. If this is an occasional accident, have a matter-of-fact attitude about the accident. Tell him that he had an accident, and he needs to take care of changing his clothes, washing himself, and cleaning anything else soiled. The other children will make fun of him, as a normal reaction. His peers are recently toilet trained. Just do not encourage them. End the scene quickly with your matter-of-fact tone to get him to clean up.

Some of the male gender at this age do need a target! That is a great idea. Some five-year-olds are shorter, for their age, and may not be able to reach the toilet. So they miss, so to speak! Others, however, are possessed by the "silly little boy syndrome." They discover that they can aim at various objects. Go ahead. Make a target. Do not allow him to develop his own!

The main thing to remember about all this is that at the age of five years, some children are still at the end of the toilet-training stage of development. All children do not reach developmental milestones at the exact average age; there is a wide range of development that is within normal range. The other key piece of information for all caregivers of children is that this part of development of toilet training is solely controlled by the child. Forcing or criticizing the child will not stop, but probably will only prolong, the accidents. As with other developmental milestones, positive reinforcement of toileting correctly will be rewarded with success!

Q

Dear Nurse Libby,

One of the things that we sometimes forget when potty training is to teach our kids how to wipe themselves properly. Do you have any suggestions on teaching children the proper way to wipe? I have always instructed my boys that they need to wipe themselves too.

However I have found that they give their penis a quick shake and that is it. Is it? What about little girls? I have always told them to wipe from front to back to avoid infection. Am I right? Also, moist tissues that can be flushed into the toilet are now on the market. Are these safe to use?

A

Dear Mrs. Kathy,

Wiping properly is very important. As I explained in the question on urinary tract infections, proper wiping can be the best defense against such an infection. You are correct in your method of teaching the children to wipe. However, little boys will need a lesson on anal wiping after a bowel movement also. The child should be taught to wipe from front to back, NOT back and forth. It doesn't matter as much for little boys, for obvious anatomical reasons, but this method adds more protection against an infection! Little boys, again due to anatomical reasons, are pretty safe with the quick shake; however, teaching them to also wipe off provides more protection.

What about little girls? You are right to teach them to wipe from front to back, especially after a bowel movement. As stated in the question on urinary tract infections, poor personal hygiene—that is, improper wiping—is the most common cause of a urinary tract infection. Proper wiping is sometimes hard to master until the child is close to, if not already, school age. So, during the training period, the trainer needs to check the results of the wiping, especially after a bowel movement!

As far as the new moist tissues that are flushable are concerned, I personally do not like them. As they state, they are moist. This moisture could set the child up for inflammation, resulting in infection. Good old toilet tissue is better, in my opinion. If the child is soiled, due to not quite making it to the bathroom in time, he or she may require a cleaning with soap and water, and then drying. For convenience, I guess one could use these wipes for this reason and then dry with regular toilet tissue or a towel. Toilet tissue can be a source of infection also, especially for the sensitive child. If the toilet tissue is scented, some children can react to the fragrance. This could result in either an inflammation or a urinary tract infection. It is probably best for you to use a nonscented brand.

Q

Dear Nurse Libby,

One of the things that should go hand in hand with toilet training is good hand-washing techniques. In my house I make the children wash their hands after using the bathroom as well as before meals and snacks, after outside play, when they blow their nose, and if they pet the animals. The children are actually pretty good at remembering to wash their hands, but they don't seem to take their time and wash them properly. Now I make each child sing a simple little song while scrubbing with the soap. Here goes . . .

"THIS IS THE WAY WE SCRUB OUR HANDS,
SCRUB OUR HANDS, SCRUB OUR HANDS.
THIS IS THE WAY WE SCRUB OUR HANDS
SO WE CAN GET RID OF GERMS."

This seems to help them concentrate on what they are doing and will hopefully help to get rid of the germs. I have truly noticed a decrease in the number of times the children have been sick since I started this. I thought you might want to share our song with some of your patients.

A

Dear Mrs. Kathy,

You have a very cute idea here with your hand-washing song. You are right that most children and some adults do not take the time to wash their hands correctly. You are also correct that proper hand washing is our first line of defense against infection! I'm not surprised that you have seen a decrease in the number of infective illnesses since starting this adorable routine.

The only thing I could add to the fact that one must wash thoroughly with soap is that after the rinsing, paper towel dry first, before turning off the faucet! And, use the towel to turn it off! Why, you may ask? Just think about it. You turn on the faucet with dirty hands full of germs. If you turn off the faucet with your nicely clean wet hands, the germs will automatically reattach themselves to your nicely clean hands. By using the towel, the germs cannot get to your nicely clean hands. This technique takes a few extra seconds and means a few extra seconds of running water, but it keeps the germ population down even more!

I will definitely pass on this song to my patients!

Imagination

Q

Dear Nurse Libby,

Kerrie (age five years) has been coming to child care telling us stories that are really outrageous. She recently told us that she found a deer in her yard with a broken leg, and that her father had put the deer in the kitchen in a box until it got better. Of course when her father arrived at the end of the day I asked him about the deer, and he had no idea what I was talking about. She also told me that she took her dog for a walk and someone shot it. She stated that her mother went out and got her a new puppy to replace the dog. When I asked her mother about the dog, she again had no idea what I was talking about. Kerrie's stories are so lifelike and filled with great detail that they are hard not to believe. Is this the sign of a great imagination or a great liar?

How should I handle these little fibs, and what should her parents do?

A

Dear Mrs. Kathy,

I feel your frustration! This is a great topic! At the age of four to six, children have a great imagination. They just don't always know how to deal with it. This is the time in life where children have the most dramatic nightmares and fears. They are starting to think abstractly. Before the age of four, most thoughts are concrete. What I mean by that is that everything is taken literally. For example, a nine-month to one-year-old child thinks that out of sight is gone. When you leave this age group to go into another room, they cry. In their mind, you are gone. As the mind develops, preschoolers start to think abstractly, to imagine. I know I went quickly from an early stage to our present concern. Think about how toddlers (one to three years old) learn the concept of parent/caregiver disappearing and returning and becoming comfortable with being left. They also become comfortable with more and more people and things. This process involves being able to think abstractly, being able to think and show feelings—something they cannot touch or be physically gratified from.

The four- to six-year-old mind is full of concrete and abstract thoughts. Think about it this way: We tell our children facts and fiction. We tell them things that are true, and then we read to them or have them watch a movie that is fiction. Their mind is developing the ability to figure out the difference. Their mind is full of fact and fiction. This is the stage of imaginary friends and developing believable stories as Kerrie is doing.

What to do about it? That is the question! The child with a great imagination is usually bright. You do not want to discourage this abstract thinking. You do want to encourage her to realize fact and fiction, though. You can tell her that she told a great story, but ask her if it is real or not. Sometimes, the child will stick to the story as being real, and for the child it is, just like imaginary friends and things in the bedroom that cause nightmares. With her parents present, you can ask her to validate the story. This will help her differentiate fact and fiction. Try to be positive about her imagination, while at the same time teaching her fact and fiction. Just remember, it is a developmental stage. If you handle it this way, she will develop to the next stage just fine. She will keep her imagination and channel it just fine.

Sex Education

Q

Dear Nurse Libby,

Cindy (age four years) approached Tommy (age five years) after school today and asked him if he would like to see her Mickey Mouse bra. His response to the question was, "Why do you need a bra? Are your breasts getting larger?"

I was surprised that at age five Tommy was aware of the purpose of a bra. Should I have intervened on this conversation, or let them continue to talk?

A

Dear Mrs. Kathy,

Your response was a normal adult response to seeing four- and five-year-olds interacting about sex differences! At four to five years of age, boys and girls are aware of body differences and are naturally curious. They very often expose themselves to each other to compare the differences. Parents and caregivers need to be aware of this developmental stage. Yes, that is what all this curiosity is—another developmental milestone for the child.

Children, obviously, should be supervised and should be encouraged to keep their bodies private; but we must supervise and encourage in a nonprovocative manner. Use a matter-of-fact approach. "Yes, boys and girls are different, but we all wear clothes to cover our bodies," could be one way to end the investigation. This generation is exposed to so much that is more advanced than their development in this area, especially through the media, that it is not surprising to hear four- and five-year-olds discussing bras! It is a healthy developmental time, as long as it is supervised.

Caregivers and parents vary on their feelings about this developmental time. Their level of comfort about their own bodies and nudity will carry over to the child. Some parents allow their children to see them nude; others always cover themselves in front of their children. The different attitudes generally are social and cultural in background. The healthiest approach for the developing five-year-old mind is the matter-of-fact approach, just like any other developmental milestone. "Yes, boys and girls have different bodies. That is what makes us either a girl or a boy" would be a statement on the five-year-old level.

The caregiver may want to share this episode with the parents of the children involved to inform them that the children are at this stage of development and to note the parents' preference on handling future investigative episodes. Cindy needs a gentle reminder that she is to keep her clothes on and not show her undergarments to everyone!

Q

Dear Nurse Libby,

Today I overheard Tommy (age six years) asking Kerrie (age five years) if she wanted to get naked and kiss him. Kerrie became very upset and called for me. I removed Tommy from the room, and I asked him what he said and why. He started to cry and would not answer me. This is not the first time he has made remarks of this nature to the children.

I am concerned about this for several reasons. First, where does a six-year-old learn about this? Second, how should I handle this situation with Tommy? Finally, how do I handle this situation with Kerrie and her parents? I feel that because she was upset about the comment, she realizes that this type of conversation is not appropriate for a child. I did make Tommy apologize, and I did call each parent at work.

A

Dear Mrs. Kathy,

This is a difficult situation to say the least. However, it is becoming more frequent I'm afraid. Where does a six-year-old come up with this stuff? Look around. Our media is sexually oriented from movies to commercials. Tommy is at a stage where he needs to become interested in other subjects. Does he ride a bike or play outdoors regularly with other boys his age? I gather from your child care profile that he is in the minority around the house during the day at least. Maybe during the day you can provide him with other interests.

You did the right thing by making Tommy apologize to Kerrie to make her feel better. The fact that he cried and showed emotion is evidence that he felt remorse or guilt for what he said. For Tommy to realize that what he did was inappropriate, you may need to go a little further. With Tommy's parents' permission, you need to set up guidelines for acceptable language and behavior while at child care. Along with trying to help Tommy develop other interests, he needs to learn to take responsibility for his actions. Teaching children to say they are sorry to another child when they can see that they hurt that child's feelings is a good social lesson. Sometimes they may not agree that their actions were necessarily wrong, but they do feel remorse for the way they made the other person feel.

You were also correct to inform Kerrie's parents about the issue. They will feel more comfortable leaving their daughter with you if you are open and honest with them. Reassure them that the situation is being handled and give them follow-up reports.

Q

Dear Nurse Libby,

After lunch today, I told Juan (age five years), Marla (age four years), and Cindy (age four years) to go into the bathroom to wash their hands. The next thing I know, I hear Juan discussing the fact that he has a penis. The girls were very interested in this. I told the children that it was time to get out of the bathroom to take naps.

When the children woke up from their naps, guess what was the first thing they talked about? That's right, Juan's penis.

Should I permit these conversations? Should I talk to the parents so that they are clear on where the use of this word came from? In this day and age, one can never be too careful.

A

Dear Mrs. Kathy,

Children, at the age of four and five years, are discovering the physical differences between boys and girls. They will undress together and look at each other's genitals in an attempt to learn about these differences. This is another developmental milestone. It is a healthy normal developmental stage.

In a child care situation, where the children are together everyday, in a relaxed home-like atmosphere, they will be more comfortable learning about their physical differences from each other. I suggest that you let the parents know what is going on and that this curiosity is normal at this age. With their permission, you could allow the conversation as long as you participate. It is important to teach the children the proper names of our genitals in a matter-of-fact way. Just like we have arms, legs, eyes, and so on, boys have a penis and girls do not! This age group may or may not ask further questions. They may be satisfied that girls do not have a penis—or they may want to know what girls have!

You may want to get some reference books that explain the differences between boys and girls at the four- to five-year-old level. The book will matter-of-factly explain body parts and why they are different. This sex education could expand to sex and pregnancy. Again, answer the question directly and honestly. There are some great resources to help you explain these important facts of life to this curious age group. They can be found at your local library. Get books that are age appropriate.

These children may occasionally expose themselves in the future. They need close supervision. Just matter-of-factly tell them, "We go in the bathroom one at a time; we keep our clothes on, and our genitals are private parts. It's okay to occasionally see someone's genitals, but not okay to touch!"

If you supervise discussions in a matter-of-fact manner, most likely these children will pass right through this developmental stage easily.

Chapter 3

LETTERS ON BEHAVIOR

Discipline Means to Teach

Q

Dear Nurse Libby,

One day, as Andy (almost one year old) was being dropped off in the morning, he started to pull over the trash can. I said, "No! That is dirty and if it falls on you it would hurt you." I picked him up and moved him to the playroom. His mother stated to me that she does not tell him "No," rather she explains that she does not want him to do whatever he is doing wrong and removes him from the situation. She felt that "No" was a negative and that he needs to hear positive.

I believe that when a child does something that could cause harm to him- or herself or someone else, a firm "No!" is warranted. In other situations, I would try to redirect the child to a positive activity.

What is you opinion on the use of the "No" word?

A

Dear Mrs. Kathy,

Developmentally, a one-year-old cannot remember tomorrow everything told to him yesterday! I believe that you are right in saying a firm "No!" to a one-year-old for doing something that could harm him or another child (like pulling something over on himself, hitting another child, or running into the street).

An active toddler could theoretically be told "No" all day long! This age is the age of exploration. The toddler is on his own, so to speak, walking independently. He doesn't know there are things that can harm him; things are not to be touched, and the like. He is just out there exploring, finding out what is in his world! If he is into something that will harm him or someone else, I agree to tell him firmly "No" and take him to something he can touch and say, "Here, play with this!" If it is something that is just untouchable to the toddler, remove him from the negative and accentuate the positive. "Here, you play with this. Oh, look at this." This is a type of discipline that uses distraction (taking him away from the harmful situation or untouchable object) and redirection (taking him to something safe and developmentally age appropriate). The theory behind this type of discipline (teaching) is that the child will learn good behavior by positive reinforcement of the accepted behavior.

After the age of two and definitely by age three, children are able to remember and start the process of learning right from wrong. With the use of the technique of positive reinforcement, distraction, and redirection of their behavior, they usually learn the rules of their society. There are some situations when toddlers and preschoolers may not respond to this technique of discipline. It may be necessary to use other methods of discipline.

Q

Dear Nurse Libby,

Children come in all different shapes and sizes, as well as different personalities. Because each child has a different personality, I have found that certain children respond to disciplinary action in different manners. When Ricky, Jenny, or Penny are put in time-out for hitting, they usually cry and appear remorseful. Other children laugh and goof off when in time-out, and as soon as they have sat for the appropriate time, they go back to doing what got them in trouble in the first place. I always discuss with them why they have been removed from the situation and placed in time-out.

It is my responsibility to make a set of rules and make sure they are followed. I however need to set up a consequence when the rules are not followed. Because time-out does not always work, are there other approaches I should try? Should the consequence be tailored toward the child or should the consequence remain the same for all?

A

Dear Mrs. Kathy,

We all need to remember that to discipline means to teach, not to punish. You do need rules at a child care center. If your rules are not followed, the children need to learn to follow them (i.e., learn to obey the rules of your child care center). If they choose not to follow the rules, they need to accept the consequences of their actions.

Let me first discuss the technique of discipline that you have used in your question—time-out. Time-out is just that, time out from society, time to think about any action that goes against the rules of that society (in this case, the child care center). This technique has rules also. First, the children are taught the rules of the child care center. They are told that if they do not follow these rules, they will go to a time-out area. While in the time-out area, the child cannot be talked to, cannot talk or verbalize, and cannot play with anything. The child has to stay in the time-out area for a designated time period. This time period is subject to the age of the child and is usually one minute per year of age. The time-out area has to be somewhat isolated from the rest of the group, but able to be observed by the caregiver. If the child doesn't show remorse in the usual fashion, it doesn't mean that he or she is not aware of or does not take responsibility for his or her actions. If the child does not observe the rules of time-out, the time is to be started again. A timer of some kind is usually set for the designated time-out. Most children don't want to be isolated from their peers, and thus will obey the time-out rules so that they can be reunited with the group. They will try to obey the rules of their society (the child care center).

The rules of the child care center must be age appropriate. They may have to be repeated daily, for each activity as needed. For example, if you were doing an art project, you would explain the directions for the project. At the same time, you would possibly talk about safety, use of scissors, crayons, and other related things. You would remind the children that if they cannot follow the rules, they go to time-out. The caregiver should discuss with the child briefly why he or she is going to time-out. Most children will already know that what they did was against the rules. They just need a time-out to get themselves back on track.

Some children, due to different maturity levels and different personalities, test the rules of the society. They may not yet be mature enough to control their impulses. Continual, consistent structure in any child's life, no matter what the maturity level, will result in teaching a child to obey rules. Some children take longer to mature than others. Just don't give up! The rewards are too great!

You did not mention the age of these children. I am assuming they are at least two years old or older. Children have to be at least two years old before they can start to remember rules, but they will not be consistent in following them. By the age of four years, they can begin to remember rules and follow them consistently. For this reason, it might be more effective to use the discipline technique that involves positive reinforcement as your primary discipline measure. This method is actually effective for a primary discipline technique for all the children. We all like to be told we are good! So, you point out the positive behavior one of the children is displaying during an activity. Follow this with pointing out another child following the rules. Most likely the rest of the children will imitate this good behavior so that they can be acknowledged and positively reinforced.

The impulsive toddler and the hyperactive child may require a little more creative discipline. If this child is not doing the accepted behavior, or is not inclined to imitate the accepted behavior, you can aid the child in the right direction. First, try ignoring the negative behavior. If you point out this negative behavior, the child might feel that the behavior is being positively reinforced. However, if you ignore the negative behavior and, at the same time, either distract the child from that behavior and/or redirect the child to a positive behavior, he or she will be positively reinforced.

If, however, a child cannot follow the rules after using this technique of positive reinforcement, ignoring, distraction, and redirection, then go to the technique of time-out. Just remember that your goal is to teach acceptable behavior and help this child to become a positive member of society. Discipline means to teach!

Q

Dear Nurse Libby,

I have found that children have three different reactions, when it comes to following the rules:

1. *Not understanding the rules, due to age or lack of information.*
2. *Understanding the rules, and choosing to follow them.*
3. *Understanding the rules, but choosing not to follow them.*

Let me give you an example:

When the twins were two years old, I would tell them to sit on the chair and wait as I checked on Robin. I would walk to the other side of the room, and they were sitting exactly as I had left them.

When Robin was two years old, I would tell her to sit on the chair and wait for me while I checked on Andy. But, as soon as I turned my back, she would get off the chair. When I returned, she did not even realize that she had done something inappropriate.

Now we have Andy, age two. When I ask him to sit and wait, as soon as my back is turned, he is off the chair and into something. The minute I turn back and ask him what he is doing, he runs back to the chair.

Because I am consistent with my child care skills, I wonder if this type of behavior is a personality disorder.

I am aware that Andy has a hard time following the rules, so I try not to set him up for failure. For instance, if I turn my back, I take him with me. However, what should I do when I do catch him doing something inappropriate? He realizes that he has done something he is not supposed to do, but he still decides to do it. Is this child headed for the road to crime?

A

Dear Mrs. Kathy,

I don't know. You have given me a loaded question this time. First of all you are discussing, probably, the most difficult age group of all—the terrible twos. The two-year-old is very self-centered. They are impulsive. They think of immediate gratification only. Everything is "me" and "mine"! They are the center of their universe. Everything revolves around them. If you watch the interactions of two-year-olds (which I am sure you have), they usually interact by biting, pulling hair, pinching, or all these (and more). They do not share. To sit still is physically impossible. This is the age of exploration! As you can see, a lot is happening at this age!

However, there is a range of normal development in this age group as in any other stage. So, you may very well have two-year-olds who are developmentally able to sit still for a period of time. I would not expect the time to be more than a few minutes. Then you can have the child who explores in a "middle of the road" sort of fashion. She doesn't get into too much trouble. Then, you have the hyperactive type. This toddler can't sit still for a minute! He has to touch everything twice! These are all examples of the two-year-old behavior.

So, to keep pace with this active toddler, you just think positive. Try to limit "No!" Instead, redirect the active toddler to an acceptable activity. Play down the non-acceptable behavior. For example: Andy is supposed to sit down for book time. Instead, he runs to the toy area and grabs a toy. You can ignore the inappropriate behavior and involve him directly with the story you are reading. Ask him to come and see the picture of the black cat.

Remember, discipline means to teach. Some toddlers respond to discipline sooner than others. What I mean by this is, as in any age group, some children are more mature than others. If the discipline technique of positive reinforcement (as described in the previous letters) does not work, then usually by age two time-out will work. Only for one minute per year though! The key is to be consistent and don't give up.

Andy may be one of the hyperactive two year olds. He can mature out of this stage also. It just may take him a little longer!

Now to your question of whether Andy is headed for a life of crime. A lot of studies have been done on the hyperactive child and criminal behavior. The impulsive characteristic of this type of child puts him at a higher risk for taking chances that could lead to a criminal life. If he were to consistently be allowed to get away with inappropriate behavior throughout his childhood, he is at a higher risk. On the other hand, sometimes, these very active little ones are the creative geniuses of the next generation. So, be consistent and don't give up on him!

Q

Dear Nurse Libby,

Tommy (age eight) was told not to touch the Christmas tree that was located in an area that was off limits in the child care. He disregarded the rules, even though his father told him. He entered the room, touched the Christmas tree, and a bulb fell off and broke.

His father had him apologize for entering the room and touching the tree. I explained to Tommy that saying "Sorry" does not excuse doing actions that one knows are inappropriate. Should his father have disciplined him for his actions?

A

Dear Mrs. Kathy,

It appears that Tommy is confused with respecting someone's wishes and being sorry for something he did (that was against someone's wishes). He seems to have little impulse control. Some children will push the limit. If Tommy's only consequence is to say he is sorry for what he did, he may feel that that is easy enough. He may choose to continue to do as he pleases.

It is not difficult to teach children to respect rules. It does take time and consistency. Children do not usually learn from a one-time experience. However, if no consequences are given to the child, it may take a long time for that child to learn respect of any rule of society. Tommy is in school now and is old enough to be responsible for his actions. I'm sure there are rules of respect for others' belongings in school.

The real issue of raising responsible, respectful children is to have consistent rules with rewards and consequences. So, even if Tommy says he is sorry, which I am sure he was, he still should have to pay a consequence. So to answer your question, yes, there should have been a consequence for his behavior.

For school age children, time-out may not be taken seriously. Remember discipline means to teach. Now would be a good time to introduce a family/child care contract.

The Family Contract

The following outline of how to structure a family/child care contract has been described in many ways. It can be very helpful to parents, caregivers, and children alike, as it allows for rules to be in place when emotions get involved. All children want and need structure to grow and mature. They learn very early how to get what they want. They learn whose buttons they can push! If rules, consequences, and rewards are in place from the beginning, there is less button pushing going on. The child learns that certain behaviors will result in either a reward or a consequence. The choice then becomes that of the child.

The first thing that has to happen is that all caregivers involved in a child's life have consistent rules. The easiest way for a contract to work is for the rules to be the same no matter who is the caregiver of the child. This is very important and so hard to accomplish! Children now live with both parents, a single parent, a grandparent(s), a guardian, or some other arrangement. Then they attend schools or child care. They may split their time between any of these combinations! If any of the combinations gives the child structure, it can only help the child.

A family contract can be started with a child as young as 3 years old. Obviously, what is written for a 3-year-old will be different than what is written for a 13-year-old! The basis of the contract is the same: respect and responsibility in the home. The caregivers write down the things they will do for the child—that is, love, feed, clothe, shelter, and support. You can elaborate on the particular aspects of how this is to be accomplished. (It is obviously more important to do this with a teenager). Next, the caregiver(s) write(s) a list of the rules for each child in the family. The rules should be written with the age of the child in mind. What I mean by that is that responsibilities, rewards, and consequences will be different for each child depending on their age and maturity level.

Let me give you an example of a family contract for a nine-year-old. The caregiver(s) will state that they will love, feed, clothe, and shelter the child. They will provide family outings and special time with the child regularly.

Child's Responsibilities

1. *Get up in the morning for school, when awakened, pleasantly.*
2. *Get ready for school in a timely manner.*
3. *Do all class work and homework and do well in school.*
4. *Set the dinner table.*
5. *Help clean room weekly.*

You can add any special chores you feel are age appropriate and needed in your family.

Rewards for Living Up to Responsibilities

1. *Extra free time, TV, computer time (time limits at caregiver's discretion)*
2. *Special events (overnight with a friend, have a friend spend the night, go to a movie, and the like)*

Consequences for Not Living Up to Responsibilities

1. *Removal of TV, computer time*
2. *Removal of privilege to go someplace special*

You can add any special consequences you feel are age appropriate and that work with your family or child care setting.

Put all this information in a contract form. Have all parties sign the contract. Keep it in a safe place. When issues arise and emotions are rising, just pull out the contract and go by what you have already agreed upon. It truly works, especially with teenagers! Extra chores can be used as a consequence (age appropriate). You can add any special rewards that are age appropriate and that work with your family or child care.

Q

Dear Nurse Libby,

One of the children, age six years old, shoved a piece of mulch inside the lock to the shed door, and I was not able to get my key into the lock to open the door. This is where I store all the equipment for outside play. I asked the children who were near the door how the mulch got into the lock. They all claimed they did not know. I took the children back inside and informed them that we would have to miss outside play. I asked them again to admit who damaged the door. No answer.

The children knew that the door to the shed was off limits. They also knew who broke the lock. I felt that by missing outside play, they would learn the consequence for their action. This could have been the front door to the child care center, and we could have been locked outside. I involved the parents in the problem, and I asked them to discuss the need for their child to confess if he or she had broken the lock or to tell me if he or she knew who did. Do you think I handled this situation appropriately?

A

Dear Mrs. Kathy,

I think you handled the situation superbly! You were probably very disappointed that (1) the lock was broken, (2) that not a single child would stand up and tell on the other child, and (3) the child him/herself would not come forward! You did the right thing to give all the children involved a time-out to regroup. The result of this time-out however, is a lesson in developmental sociology. These children are together everyday. From your profile, I'm guessing the ones involved are mostly between 7 and 11 years old. They play and probably disagree together everyday. This age group devotes most of their energies to peer group interactions and acceptance. They are moving away from the protective arms of the adult caregiver in their lives. They are equals in that they are all the children with you as the caregiver adult. Therefore, if they are asked to tell on one of their own, they will probably not do it. They will protect the identity of the guilty one to protect their individual identity in the group of children. I hope this makes sense to you.

By letting the parents know what happened, you let the children know that this is not over with yet. Someone broke the lock and has to be responsible for the act—especially because you had already made it a rule not to play with the lock. Most likely, in the privacy and protection of their own home, at least one person will come forward with the answer. Perhaps even the guilty one may be encouraged to be honest, when not in the presence of peers. Just like the witness protection program, the identity of the child who tells on another child should be protected. This age is a fragile social society, yet everyone must obey rules and learn to tell the truth.

If and when you find out who broke the lock, you still have some issues to deal with. First, the issue of breaking a rule of your child care must be met with a consequence. You could have the child pay outright for the repair, or you could have the child do some kind of chores while at child care to compensate for the money. If the guilty child comes forward, remembering the sociology lesson, you could show how proud you are that he or she was able to admit to the action and go a little lighter on the consequence. If another child exposes the guilty party, that child's identity, obviously, has to be protected. The consequence for the guilty one would then be a little harsher. The lesson of "honesty is the best policy" has to be given to all the children at this time. Hopefully, the parents of the offending child will offer to pay for the lock to be fixed, and they can determine the appropriate consequence for the child at home also.

Everyone was given a time-out to allow time for the truth to come out. Sometimes, it takes longer than other times for the lesson to be learned. Everyone must learn that lesson of "honesty is the best policy." We parents and caregivers have the everlasting job of teaching the younger generation. We have to remember to use the tools of our own experiences and use ourselves as examples of how to be productive and happy members of society. This is our long-term goal for our children!

Adjusting to Child Care

Q

Dear Nurse Libby,

I have a little girl (age four years) who will be joining child care next week. The parents would like to bring the child a few hours a day until she adjusts to the new surrounds. Do you feel that the child needs an adjustment period? If so, how long?

A

Dear Mrs. Kathy,

Children are really resilient. Most of them, at almost any age, can adjust to change. So for the most part the new child may not need a breaking-in period. Some children, though, may need this. As with adults, children have varying personalities. The shy, more reserved child, for example, may need shorter periods of time at the child care center in the beginning. A child who has been to a lot of different centers in a short period of time may also need a breaking-in period. A child who has recently moved to the area and to whom everything is new may also benefit from a breaking-in period.

So for a guideline, I would say that most children would do fine from the first day. However, if you encounter a child who is experiencing one of the scenarios just described, or any other issue causing them emotional stress, you should discuss with the parents a possible breaking-in period. This may include the parent staying for a few hours on the first day. Sometimes, if the parent feels secure with the child care center, then the child can feel that same security and adjust more easily. If that is not possible, you have a choice to make. You can take the child and work with him or her to develop a sense of security with your child care center. Most children will adjust to consistency in their lives; it is just a matter of time. However, if the child does not adjust after a period of time, most likely a month, you may have to tell the parent that you cannot keep the child. This is true especially if the child causes disruptions that affect the other children already under your care.

On a personal note, I will describe a reassuring scenario for you. One of my own sons was 15 months old when I needed child care for him. He was a very hyperactive toddler! I took him for the interview with the prospective child care mom. She already had two other 15-month-old toddlers in her care. We were outside in her yard trying to talk and allowing my son and her to interact. All I seemed to do was chase him around the yard. After we were back home, she called me stating she wasn't sure she could take him! She was afraid she could not handle him! I, being a mom and needing to work, was devastated. She could feel my devastation! She suggested that she keep my son for a day or two before making the final decision. She had never refused to care for a child before. Well, he was perfectly behaved for her from day one! He even became her favorite! (which hopefully the other children were not aware of). What this scenario suggests is that each child is different and should be considered on an individual basis.

Emotional Security

Q

Dear Nurse Libby,

I make a point of praising the children throughout the day for things that they do right. Recently, I have noticed that whenever I praise someone in front of Kerrie (age five years), she responds with, "What about me?" Therefore, if I tell Marla that I like the picture she colored, or that Ricky did a great job cleaning up, Kerrie wants praise too.

Sometimes I turn the question back on her by saying, "I don't know, how do you think your coloring looks?" Or "I don't know, do you think you did a good job cleaning up too?" This way I do not take anything away from the other children. How would you approach the situation?

A

Dear Mrs. Kathy,

You pretty much answered your own question! You are right in saying that all children deserve praise when they do something well. As a matter of fact, adults like and need praise also. Think about the workplace. When one adult gets a promotion or raise (praise), the rest of the staff is at least a little bit envious. We, as adults, use other words sometimes, but we essentially ask, "What about me?"

A four- to six-year-old is still developing emotional security. They are also learning and mastering all kinds of skills: like coloring in the lines, printing letters and numbers, and remembering the names of all these things (colors, numbers, and letters). They need and want praise all the time. They are so proud of everything they do. This age group is the most enthusiastic about learning than any other age group! This is the age that most wants to please adults in their lives. Sometimes, if they are not given praise, they (like us) become discouraged and don't try anymore.

In Kerrie's case, I think you should find something for which to praise her, especially if the children are doing the same activity. If you are specific about the praise of each child, you won't take anything away from the other children. For example, you could praise Marla for staying in the lines of the tree she colored, Ricky for coloring a pretty blue sky, and Kerrie for coloring the apples so red.

Sibling Rivalry

Q

Dear Nurse Libby,

I am happy to announce that Ricky's (almost four years old) mommy is going to have a baby. The baby is due in two months on Ricky's birthday. Recently I have noticed major changes in Ricky's behavior, and I am wondering if this is due to the arrival of a new sibling. He has gone from a happy-go-lucky little boy to a whining unhappy child. He does not listen to the rules and is very stubborn about every request he is given. Are there any easy ways to prepare a child for the arrival of a new family member?

A

Dear Mrs. Kathy,

The direct answer to your question is yes. There are ways to prepare a child for the arrival of a new baby. However, I'm not sure that all of Ricky's behavior changes are associated with becoming a big brother. The behaviors you are describing can be a typical four-year-old who is NOT about to become a big brother. Being a four-year-old is the last phase of babyhood. This is also the first phase of the school age child. An easy way to think about what they are going through is to think of the early adolescent years. If you can remember, it is a time of sometimes being a child and sometimes wanting to act grown-up. Well, being a four-year-old, sometimes referred to as the frustrating fours, is a time of wanting to be treated as a baby and sometimes wanting to do things on one's own. Four-year-olds have been described as two-year-olds with a mouth. At the age of four, Ricky has most likely mastered feeding himself, toileting himself, possibly even dressing himself. These are all "big boy" achievements. He should be able to share and take turns in his social environment. As I previously stated, he is approaching school age. There is no turning back! Just like the adolescent, though, he gets feelings of uneasiness about all this responsibility. So, he falls back on his comfort zone of babyhood. That is where the emotional back-and-forth comes from.

Along with the stubbornness, sometimes the four-year-old starts "back talking." Yes, it can start this early. They are testing the caregiver. They are asserting some independence on this path to school age. They are making their own decisions about some things. Their decision may or may not agree with the caregiver—which can provoke their frustration and yours. They obviously cannot be allowed to have it their way all the time. However, this is the age where if it really doesn't matter, let them make some decisions. An example of where it really doesn't matter in the scheme of things is to allow the four-year-old to pick out his or her clothes sometimes. They may not match, but it is a learning process.

I realize that at child care, where there are rules, he must follow your rules. You will most likely have to use time-out more frequently with Ricky for a while. Continued structure and consistency will prevail with this little frustrated four-year-old.

Added to his becoming four, he is to become a big brother. There are ways to make this transition easy for Ricky. His parents need to include him in as much of the planning and anticipation as possible. They should ask his help in setting up the baby's room. They should not, however, put in toys that he played with without asking his permission. He will most likely give these baby toys to his new sibling, but the idea is for Ricky to do it. It helps him to feel good about growing up. If he refuses, let him keep the toy. He will give it up in his own time. During these times, they should display praise for Ricky's "big boy" achievements to reassure him of their love for their big boy. Some children fear that they are being replaced by the new sibling, and if only they were smaller there would be no need for this new sibling! When taking Ricky shopping for the new baby, it is a good idea to reward him with something small that encourages his big boy activities. They can talk with him about how important he will be as a big brother. He, who has already learned so many things, can help his new sibling to grow up too! When the new baby arrives, if they play down the baby and play up the big brother, he will feel more secure and the baby won't mind at all sharing the limelight.

Selective Vomiting

Q

Dear Nurse Libby,

On four separate occasions, Tommy (almost six years old), has eaten so much food that he threw up as soon as he left the table. Today we were having a picnic in the kitchen, and Tommy ate several grapes and graham crackers. He stood up and walked to the corner of the kitchen and vomited in his hands. He did not attempt to run to the bathroom because I do not think that he realized that he was going to vomit. Is this something to be concerned about?

A

Dear Mrs. Kathy,

Tommy's behavior, as you describe it, is not normal. Because this has happened only four times over the course of a year, I am not too concerned. Watch Tommy eat. Is he gulping everything down very fast? As we discussed previously in the letters on toilet training, he is the same child who wet himself instead of taking the time to go to the bathroom. This could be another sign of him being impulsive. If he appears to gulp down his food, he is probably not chewing it up first and swallowing a lot of air at the same time. The air has to leave the stomach. With food on top of the air, the food will leave the stomach also!

If he is eating too fast, gulping down everything, limit his amounts of food and teach him to chew more slowly and more thorougly. The foods you describe in your letter are snack foods. Does he do this with regular meals as well? He may be trying to eat too fast the things that taste good! If this is so, teach him to savor the flavor and chew more slowly. He may be getting too much sugar at one time. Some children cannot digest sugar easily. I suggest that you limit his sweets and that you watch him eat! If that does not do the trick, send me further information.

Q

Dear Nurse Libby,

I wanted to follow up on Tommy. I have observed him eating, and you are right. He does gulp down the snack foods, not the meals. I have reminded him to chew his food slowly and to take his time when he eats. Also, I give him a small piece of fruit or one cracker and make him pace himself with the other children. Great advice, thanks.

Group Activities

Q

Dear Nurse Libby,

Because my child care consists of eight children ranging in age from six weeks to school age, I have a very structured program. The children normally have lessons and crafts at certain times throughout the morning. I normally have all the children participate in the activities in some way or another. I encourage the older children to assist the younger children. I have a five-year-old who does not want to participate in the lessons and crafts. He stated that he would rather play with the toys. I explained to him that this is not toy time, that this is lesson time. He stated that he is allowed to do what he wants at home so he should be allow to do what he wants at child care. He is in kindergarten, and I assume he is expected to participate in group activities there. Since you are familiar with a child's maturity level, do you feel that this is an age-appropriate behavior?

I would like to add that the lessons consist of fun activities like painting, coloring, puppet shows, play dough, story time, and learning letters and numbers. I keep the lessons short (15 to 20 minutes). Do you agree that I should require him to participate in the lessons or should I let him do what he wants to do?

A

Dear Mrs. Kathy,

In a home child care center with one provider to eight children, it is imperative that you are able to watch all the children at the same time. Therefore I agree with your decision to encourage him to participate in the activities at the time. At the age of five years old, he does attend kindergarten and is learning to participate as a member of a group. He may not be as mature or have the impulse control of other children his age. These group activities, with children of various ages, will aid in his development to be able to function in a group. Each child is learning to get along with other children of varying ages. They are each being exposed to various developmental levels. The older child will naturally help the younger. The younger child will naturally learn from the older child. These joint activities will teach each child important social skills. They will learn that people are different. It will teach tolerance and acceptance of others! They will also learn that as a person, each must obey the rules of society and your child care center.

Big child care centers have a different situation available. They have additional staff and normally have stations/interest centers set up so that the children can do what they choose. However, there are also set times for eating, napping, and other activities that all the children need to participate in.

Mealtime Rules

Q

Dear Nurse Libby,

When I started my child care I always allowed the children to leave the table as soon as they where finished eating. More and more I began to notice that as soon as one child declared he was done eating, everyone else was stating the same. They, however, had an entire plate of food left. I started a new policy that one could not leave the table until everyone was finished. In doing so, I began to realize that the children where not rushing through the meal and throwing away a plate of food. I even include the little ones in high chairs in this. When they are finished and start to fidget, I tell them in a soft voice that they need to wait. Then I clean their chair, wipe their hands and face, and give them a wooden spoon and a plastic bowl to play with until the meal is over. I have found that starting this at an early age makes them better eaters and better at relaxing while eating.

A

Dear Mrs. Kathy,

I found your rules for meal times quite interesting. I wish to take it a little further, as far as the family is concerned. In the hectic, sometimes rushed lifestyles we live, we are losing some basics for good health and happiness. Mealtime is not only a time of nourishment for our bodies; it is a social time as well. If we all were held to your policy, we would eat slower, chewing our food more, which is better for our digestion. We would probably eat a more balanced meal. We would probably interact with the members of our families more.

I know that the dinner meal is the most convenient meal for this interaction to take place. If all families sat together until everyone finished eating, there would be some interesting dialogue in houses all over the country!

Shyness

Q

Dear Nurse Libby,

Paul (age 20 months) has been with me since he was 12 months. Prior to that time he stayed at home with his mother. He is the youngest of three children, the oldest being 14, the middle child being 8. Paul is very shy. Even after watching him for six months, he has a difficult time making eye contact. When I go to change his diaper, he sometimes tries to kick me. When I hold him in my arms, he looks the other way. When other parents arrive, he will start to cry and then, and only then, does he hold on to me. When his father brings him in the morning, he holds on to his father's leg until I pick him up. Then he cries until his father is gone. When his mother arrives at night, he comes over to me and refuses to let go of me. When I place him in the playroom with the other children, he will sit on the floor and whine for about 15 minutes or longer. Then he may get off the floor and grab a toy and hide. He still does not speak. Only within the last week has he started to say "ma." Is this typical behavior for a shy child or is he possibly delayed in his development or both?

A

Dear Mrs. Kathy,

Paul may be just severely shy, or he may indeed be developmentally delayed. You state he has been with you since he was 12 months old. He is now 8 months older. He should have adjusted to you and the other children by now. The lack of eye contact bothers me. Even infants give you eye contact. It is one of the first signs of development. An infant will look at another face and smile back.

This toddler should be able to give eye contact. He probably should be saying at least a few more words at 20 months old. Does he understand and follow commands? For instance, can he pick up a toy and put it in a designated place? If he can do this, he can follow a complex command. That would show he is mentally okay. He may have a communication disorder. He may have an emotional disorder. Paul is in dire need of a full evaluation. You say his mother does not see problems in his behavior. She is probably in denial. It is sometimes hard to admit that you have a child with a delay.

You can help him in a lot of ways. You can be consistent with his routine. The average two-year-old becomes somewhat ritualistic in behavior. They like things to stay the same. For example, the two-year-old likes family members to always sit in the same seat at the dinner table. They get highly upset if someone changes this arrangement. They may like the same routine for nap and bedtime. No one else may be able to put them to bed without a fight. This behavior usually passes as they approach three years old.

As far as his shyness and lack of eye contact go, these are harder to help. You can be consistent in making sure you give him eye contact when you talk to him. Touch him when you talk to him. Touching can make him feel comfort and hopefully ease him into developing trust. Some children are extremely shy and will not go after what they want. He may be THAT shy. Give him a few toys that are just for him for a little while. After a week or two, see whether he becomes secure enough to be in the group of children. You must remember, the two-year-old cannot share, nor do they play with other children. If he is indeed very shy, he may also lack the security to interact.

If Paul does not show any changes for the better in a month or two, I urge you to continue to talk with his parents. In your situation, being with him most of the day, you could also document his behavior. Then, as a concerned and caring caregiver, sit down with his parents. Hopefully they will be able to see that you are trying to get help for their son. Good luck! Let me know how Paul progresses.

Separation Anxiety

Q

Dear Nurse Libby,

Paul has been in my care since he was one year of age. He is with me almost fifty hours a week. He will be two years old next month. Since he was 18 months old, he has been very aggressive toward me. When his father comes to drop him off, Paul starts with screaming and holding on to his father's leg. I try to reach out to him, but he tries to punch me or pull my hair. When his father leaves, Paul will sit on the floor and scream, sometimes for an hour. If I try to sit with him or talk to him, it upsets him even worse. This has been going on for almost six months now. The child is obviously not happy here, and this situation is making the morning very stressful for all of us. I have decided that the family will need to seek child care elsewhere because this situation is to stressful for everyone.

The child is very shy and normally does not relate well to the other children. I am also concerned because he does not talk or make eye contact with me. He does calm down in the morning, and then he wants me to hold him for the rest of the day. If I sit with him and then need to leave him to assist another child, he begins to cry again. He has also been striking out at his mother and his sister. He is very aggressive with the other children in child care as well.

I feel that he would be better suited for a nanny because of his shyness and his need for one-on-one care. Perhaps someone coming to his house would be less stressful than him leaving. I would also like to add that this is very painful for me. In a way I feel like a failure, and truthfully the decision to let him go was more so because of the disruption that occurs. The older children go to school stressed out because of the morning events. I find it difficult to make breakfast and spend time with the other children because I am so consumed with Paul.

A

Dear Mrs. Kathy,

This situation is a very complex one. Paul, at the age of two years, is in the peak age group for separation anxiety. This is a normal developmental stage of fear of separation from the parent. At this stage of development, the child has bonded with the parents and is afraid that if they leave, they will never come back. Out of sight is gone for good in their mind. However, the child usually becomes more secure each time the parent returns and the same scenario is repeated. Because Paul has been with you for almost a year now, he normally should have adjusted to the routine of being with you for fifty hours a week.

The next thing that bothers me is the degree of his reaction. The screaming for an hour on a regular basis for almost six months is not a normal separation anxiety. Most children, going through this phase, cry until the parent leaves, and then adjust soon thereafter to the routine of the day. I am also concerned about his interactions with people. His lack of giving people eye contact is not normal. He is also delayed in speech development. Paul deserves a complete work-up. He may have a neurological developmental condition and could be helped with treatment. The earlier the diagnosis is made, the better the prognosis (the chances for achieving developmental normalcy).

I agree with you that possibly Paul would do better at home in a one-on-one situation. He surely isn't thriving in child care with a lot of people. So don't agonize over your decision.

Q

Dear Nurse Libby,

Andy seems to scream and cry whenever I walk away from him. This happens even if I am a few feet away and still in eyeshot. It has gotten so bad that I try to sneak past him to go into the kitchen to make the kids lunch. The area in my home where I do child care is one large room. There are no walls or dividers, so the children can see me at all times. Even though he can still see me, he screams when he realizes I am not next to him. He also cries when I pick him up and then put him down to change his diaper, place him in the high chair, and when he runs out of food. This was not always the case. This behavior started a few months ago, and I have noticed that it is worse when he has been with his grandmother the day before. His parents have complained about the same behavior. He stays with his grandmother twice a week, and I assume that she gives him one-on-one attention and perhaps holds him throughout the day.

A

Dear Mrs. Kathy,

Andy is going through separation anxiety. All children go through this stage. It usually starts around six months of age. It can continue and reoccur through the toddler years (until age three). Andy has to differentiate his surroundings at least twice a week. This complicates things for him and for you!

With two different caregivers, there will be two different routines he must fit into! His grandmother may be holding him all the time. That will complicate his adjustment to your routine, naturally. You need to discuss this further with his parents. They need to find out what is happening at Grandmother's house and make a decision, if they can, to have Andy stay at one place. If that is not possible, then maybe Grandmother, you, and the parents can agree on a routine for Andy that is similar no matter where he is. He may still cry if you are not close on and off, but this cooperation between caregivers will lessen his anxiety!

Q

Dear Nurse Libby,

As soon as Samantha (age one year) sees her mother coming to pick her up at the end of the day, she starts to scream and cry. Samantha's mom comments on how bad this reaction to her feels, and although I try to reassure her that it is better to have them crying when they are leaving instead of crying when they are coming, I still see how hurt she is. We tried sitting down and talking for 10 minutes before picking her up and taking her home, but she still screams. Samantha's mom is pregnant and is finding it difficult to lift and carry her. She also states that when her husband comes home from work, Samantha pushes her away and wants nothing else to do with her. Any suggestions?

A

Dear Mrs. Kathy:

Samantha's situation is a very delicate one. She is going through separation anxiety. This is a developmental milestone, which occurs between 6 and 15 months of age. The baby realizes who familiar persons are and who are strangers. Samantha's comfort zone is with her caregiver, though, and not with her mother. Although this is a good thing for Samantha and you, it is a difficult time for Samantha and her mother. But it must be reassuring to her mother that Samantha is in good hands.

Samantha could be reacting to her mother's limitations, so to speak. The pregnancy is very tiring and possibly anxiety producing. Samantha is intuitive enough at this age to pick up her mother's anxiety and pull away from it.

You are right in sitting down with her mother, to allow Samantha time to switch gears to her mother. The fact that Samantha is fine with her father, though, gives me cause for concern. It appears to be a deeper emotional issue for Samantha and the mother. You probably could suggest that Samantha's mother seek professional advice from Samantha's primary care provider (doctor, nurse practitioner, or physician's assistant) and mother's obstetrical provider (doctor or nurse midwife).

Sometimes it is difficult for mothers to work and have someone else be the primary caregiver (which a child care mother is, essentially). Sometimes this situation can cause unconscious anxiety and unconscious neglect of the child. The child will cling to the caregiver of most comfort. Hopefully, this situation will improve, especially because this mother will soon have two babies to care for and nurture.

Q

Dear Nurse Libby,

When Marla arrived today, she was crying that she did not want her mother to leave. Marla will soon be five years old. I notice this behavior more often after she has been with her father over the weekend. Her mother gets very agitated and tells her if she does not "knock it off, Mrs. Kathy will get angry, and put you in time-out!" I am sure that the mother tells her this to make her stop crying, but this makes the situation worse, and it makes me the heavy. I normally ask her to help me set up for breakfast. This diversion often helps to dry her tears. I am wondering why this occurs after the weekends with her father. Could it be that she simply is reacting to the lack of time she spends with her mom? I hope she is not being placed in the middle of the divorce. I want to make Marla's Monday less stressful, and I do not want to be the heavy in the situation. What should I do?

A

Dear Mrs. Kathy,

I agree with you! You should not be made the heavy in this situation. However, Marla should not be the heavy either. If she acts more upset after being away from her mother and being with her father for the weekend, there may be more to this than just not wanting her mother to leave.

Sometimes, children are put in the middle of their parents' problems. Divorce has increased, as we all know. This epidemic has resulted in a lot of children splitting their time between their parents. They have a lot of changes to adjust to! These changes alone can cause emotional issues for the child. If the parents have continued issues, they sometimes involve the child. The child may feel that he or she needs to take care of the parent.

I don't know if this is the case with Marla, but there sure are some signs pointing that way. The fact that she is teary after a weekend with her father is a big sign. She either just misses her mother too much, or some emotional entanglements are there.

I would advise you to discuss this behavior with her mother. She may not notice the time issue. Let her know that you have observed this behavior after the weekends Marla has been away from her. See how Marla's first hours back are with her mother. Maybe Marla gets back just in time to go to bed for the night. Marla obviously needs a little time to enjoy being home with her mother before the week begins. You could gently suggest such an arrangement. During the talk with her mother, you can bring up the other issue. In the best interest of Marla, you would feel better if you were not involved in the separation issue. You are Marla's caregiver during the week. She needs to feel comfortable with you. She needs to know that you are separate from the parents in your role in her life. You can suggest that because Marla gets upset after the weekend with her dad, you hope, in the best interest of Marla, that the parents discuss this behavior. They may be able to figure out the reason and alleviate it. This opening will give you much information about the relationship of Marla's parents. You should be able to discover whether there are real issues for Marla or that she just misses her mom! Good luck!

Impulsivity

Q

Dear Nurse Libby,

Penny (age three years) has been trying to leave the area where we are playing to go and sit alone. I have watched her to see how far she would go, and she actually went to the front door to leave. I stopped her and asked her where she was going, and she said she wanted to play outside. Do you think that because she is a twin and she shares most of her time with her sister, she wanted a little space?

A

Dear Mrs. Kathy,

Some children are more impulsive than others. It has nothing to do with her being a twin. This type of child will try anything twice. What I mean is that most children, by the time they are three years of age, follow the rules of the house. They want to please and do so. They have just left the stage of babyhood. This age is most usually the time of the "trusting threes". So, you are right to be concerned about Penny.

As I already stated, some children are impulsive. They do not think before they act. They just do what ever comes to mind. This is not an excuse for their behavior, just an explanation. They require more structure than the average child both at the child care center and at home. Make the rules short and to the point. Let her know there will be rewards for obeying the rules and consequences for NOT obeying. Time-out is a good consequence for a three-year-old. Penny may have to spend more of her day in time-out to be able to control her impulse to go wherever she wants when she wants. You will have to be more aware of where she is for a while. This will take time, until Penny remembers how that particular impulse to leave results in the consequence of time-out.

Q

Dear Nurse Libby,

Tommy (age six years) has finally started first grade, and he is having quite a difficult time adjusting. He has had several notes from the teacher sent home and several trips to the principal's office. He gets off the bus several times a week crying and saying that the other children are picking on him. I feel so bad for him. Can you give me advice on how to handle situations at the elementary-school level?

1. *Should parents go to the school to handle a problem involving their child or should they wait and see whether the child can solve it on his or her own?*
2. *What do you say to a child who gets off the school bus in tears because someone is picking on him or her?*

I have always encouraged the children at child care to keep theirs hands to themselves. This is difficult for them to do when someone hits them first. Any suggests for this one?

A

Dear Mrs. Kathy,

Tommy sure is having a hard time! First grade can be a huge adjustment for anyone. When he does not get this support of his behavior, he probably feels abandoned; therefore the tears start flowing. Tommy is now in the situation of real school, where the rules apply to all. If he normally gets his way, school can be quite an adjustment. Let me try to give you some guidance for the situations you have described.

1. Parents going to the school whenever there is a problem is probably not a good idea. However, it depends on the severity of the problem. Obviously, if another child hurt the child, the school officials need to be aware. (I'm sure you realize violence has increased in the schools recently.) The parents are the child's best advocate. The parents should evaluate the situation, though, before contacting the school. They must realize that the story they are getting is the interpretation of the child. There are always two sides to every story. The parents should discuss the particular situation with the child, offering insight and suggestions on how Tommy can resolve the situation. They should discuss the rules of the school as they apply to each situation. They should include the fact that there are usually 20 or more children in the class, and they all have different ideas about rules and school, especially in first grade. The main thing they should discuss with Tommy is that the teacher is the boss in the classroom. The teacher makes the rules of the classroom, and everyone has to follow them no matter what they think about the rules. They could also discuss how this is the same as at the child care center.

2. The child who gets off the school bus in tears because someone is picking on him or her is already responding to being picked on. At this moment he needs reassurance. I would suggest saying nothing to him verbally. Walk with him, possibly with your arm on his shoulder or even holding his hand. After you are back at the house—child care center—you can talk to him to find out what happened. During the discussion, ask him how he could have done or said something different to prevent the incident from happening. Tommy needs to realize that he is responsible for his behavior. By asking his involvement to prevent these occurrences, Tommy will start assuming responsibility for his behavior. This is a normal developmental stage—to learn that certain behaviors get certain responses from one's peers as well as adults.

3. It is obviously NEVER good to suggest that a child hits back. You would be teaching him that hurting someone is okay. The child should tell the responsible adult that he or she was hit and let the adult discipline the offender. However, sometimes, especially with little boys, they will get into fights. Usually, it is just a

hit back and forth to settle the issue. Usually, they become good buddies after the incident. This behavior is gender related, as I stated. Boys are physically different from girls. The physical differences become more evident around four to six years of age. Boys are usually more aggressive and physical. They run, jump, and are generally more on the go than most girls. Not to say that girls are not as active. Becoming physical with each other is part of this stage. However, they must learn that hitting anyone is not accepted in our society. They need to be taught to channel their energy and competitiveness into positive activities—for example, sports.

Q

Dear Nurse Libby,

*When coming back from the bus stop today, Tommy (age five years) yelled to me, "Hurry up and open the god**** door!"*

What I did was tell him that we did not use that word here and that I did not want to hear it again. When we were alone, I told him I did not approve of the use of that language. I also called his mother to discuss the situation with her. Should I notify the other parents just in case this word gets repeated at home? I do not want them to think that I was the one who said it.

A

Dear Mrs. Kathy,

Five-year-old, outgoing boys sure can keep us on our toes! Hopefully, the call to his mother went well. His parents should be aware of and follow up on his behavior. He is learning these words somewhere, and the parents need to help (discipline) teach him proper behavior and respect.

If this episode was an isolated incident, I don't feel that you need to tell the other parents, unless you have a practice to tell them everything that happens everyday.

If Tommy develops a habit of this behavior, then definitely discuss with the other parents that you have this problem. Reassure them that you are working on it with the child and his parents, and hopefully their children will not repeat the word. See what their thoughts and ideas are to help the situation.

Q

Dear Nurse Libby,

Tommy (age seven years) is still using foul language. He will call the other children cuss words and names. I have discussed this situation again with his mother, and she states he is learning the words at school. She also informed me that she has made several trips to the school this year because of his inappropriate behavior. I am truly concerned for Tommy.

Dear Nurse Libby,

I wrote to you a while back about Tommy who was then five or six being so engrossed in an activity that he wet his pants. He is now close to seven, and he is still wetting his pants. Again it is during times when he is in the middle of something and does not want to stop. The odd thing is that if I did not detect that his pants were wet, he would walk around in them all day. I discussed this problem with his mother, and she did admit that it happens at home as well. This occurs two and three days in a row. I have asked him why he does it, thinking that maybe he has a condition that requires medical attention, and he states that he does not want to stop playing. Please tell me there is something I can do to help him.

Dear Nurse Libby,

I recently read a book about the love languages that children speak: hearing, touching, time spent, and so on. Since I have read this book, I have applied it to my children, and it is amazing. Some children respond to hearing praise, whereas others would feel love through a hug. I have noticed that Tommy tells me numerous times a day that he loves me. He tells me this when I let him have his favorite snack or I let him go outside to play or when I take him to the playground. The problem is that it does not feel genuine to me. I truly do not know how to respond to him. In the beginning I would say it back to him, sometimes I would say thank you, and sometimes I would ask him why he loved me and he would say nothing back. I feel that he says it to reward me for letting him do what he wants. Please do not get me wrong, I enjoy being told that I am loved, but I am not sure how to respond to it because sometimes it makes me feel manipulated. I do not want him to feel insecure, so I want to make sure that my response fits his need.

A

Dear Mrs. Kathy,

Tommy has many behavior issues. It appears though that the issues are becoming more frequent and severe. I have taken the liberty to combine your three most frequent accounts of Tommy's inappropriate behavior. By doing so, I hope to explain how I see Tommy.

First, and most important, Tommy deserves a complete history and physical examination. Any medical reason for his persistent and frequent daytime urinary accidents needs to be ruled out. If there is no medical reason for this condition, and with the other behaviors as symptoms, Tommy is at risk for some behavior disorders. Attention deficit/hyperactivity is the most common one. Lack of impulse control (as described in your three accounts of inappropriate behavior) is a major component of this disorder.

He is in school now, where he is exposed to the rules of the class. He is taught the rules and consequences of not obeying them. It is not normal to continue to wet his pants. It is not normal for him to constantly cuss repeatedly. It is not normal for him to constantly cause disruptions in the classroom to the point his parents have to frequent the school. It is not normal for a child to make you feel that his overt jesters of caring are not genuine. I feel Tommy is asking for help through his behavior. A seven-year-old doesn't wake up and say, "I'm going to get into so much trouble today that Mom will have to come to school." A seven-year-old doesn't wake up and say, "I'm going to wet my clothes today and just stay in them." A seven-year-old doesn't wake up and say, "I'm going to say a lot of cuss words to get myself in so much trouble today that no one will be happy."

Again, I suggest you have meetings set up with the parents to discuss child care issues and each child. Having a meeting with Tommy's parents in a relaxed, appointed time, will help them hear about their child and give their full attention. Together, maybe you and they can set up a plan of action to help Tommy.

Q

Dear Nurse Libby,

Matthew (age seven) has been taking things that to not belong to him, without asking. While at the public playground the other day, he took a scooter that belonged to someone he did not know. I asked Matthew whether he had asked permission to touch the scooter, and he said no and threw it on the ground. When we returned to my child care center, he was still upset. He hid in a corner and tore a hole in a stuffed bear and dumped the stuffing in the corner. When I asked him what he was doing, he said he did not know. When I went over to him and saw what he did, I asked him why he destroyed the bear. Again the response was that he did not know. I handed him a broom and a dustpan and had him clean up the mess. Then I asked him to sit in time-out and think about his actions. What can I do to help Matthew with his impulsive behavior?

A

Dear Mrs. Kathy,

Impulsive behavior is very hard to change and very hard to control. That is why it is called impulsive! The definition of impulsive is spontaneous; impetuous; unreflecting. The child does not think before he acts! I am not trying to give you excuses for Matthew, just trying to give you understanding. You can never let up your guard with them. They do better with structure and control. Matthew will do better with few choices.

When he does something he is not supposed to do, like the examples you have given, you must be consistent with your discipline as you have been. Remember, discipline means to teach, not to punish. Time-out will work over the long run. A child who is impulsive can only remember and tolerate small doses of rules. You must consistently remind him of the rules for the moment before he is out of your sight! I know this may sound difficult, especially when you have other children to watch, but it will work!

Sometimes the impulsive behavior interferes with the child's school and social skills. They seem to not think before any action is taken. These children will have difficulty paying attention, may fall behind in their school work, and become either the class clown or the troublemaker. These children deserve a work-up for attention deficit/hyperactivity disorder. Their primary care provider will do a complete physical and neurological examination. They may be referred to a child psychologist for a complete psychological examination with projective studies. This examination evaluates the child for any medical or learning disabilities that can be initiating the impulsive behavior. I would advise Matthew's parents to have him evaluated if this behavior continues. The treatment could make a world of difference for Matthew and everyone else in his world!

Toddler Fighting

Q

Dear Nurse Libby,

Recently, the twins (2½ years) have been fighting with each other. Usually, the fight is over a toy that one played with earlier in the day, and then went to play with something else. As soon as the other twin touches that toy, the first twin wants it back. I normally say that if you leave it, you lose it. Or should it be "I had it first?"

I also have duplicates of some of the girls' favorite toys so that they can parallel play. This, though, has also resulted in their fighting, when one of the girls wants and takes both toys!

A

Dear Mrs. Kathy,

The twins, at 2½ years of age, are in a developmental stage that is more complex, due to the fact that they are twins! At the age of 2 to 3 years, children are able to play together, but not really. They actually play beside each other, are aware of each other, and are learning to share. From birth through toddlerhood (age 1 to 2 years), babies are aware of themselves first. They are the center of their universe. Their needs are met first and foremost (in their minds).

As the toddler approaches the age of 2 and 3 years old, they are learning that there are other people in the world. They want to be around these other people, but may not want to interact or share with them all the time. These other people have needs also, and sometimes their needs are met first. This is the developmental stage of learning to share, to take turns, and to play interactive games. This development is complicated enough for a 2- to 3-year-old. For the twins, it is more so. They have had each other around all their lives. One would think that sharing should be easier for them. By the nature of being a twin, they may have a stronger need to be independent and in charge. They are, however, old enough to start the process of learning to share and respect others. Either of the rules you choose is okay, as long as you are consistent with the one you choose. The only exception should be for personal items of each twin. Duplicate toys are a great idea and will help these toddlers progress from parallel play to the stage of sharing.

Q

Dear Nurse Libby,

Ricky (age 3 years) has recently started to hit and push the other children. His prime targets are the twins (age 2½) and Robin (age 18 months). Most of the time, these attacks are prompted because someone took something that he wanted. He is an only child and usually follows what everyone is doing. I thought that because he is a follower, he would be quick to potty train. At this point he has no interest. He has become more aggressive toward the girls, and I have tried time-out, but he seems to enjoy it. I started a report card, where he gets a sticker for every two hours he goes without hitting someone, and so far the whole first sheet is empty. What can I do?

A

Dear Mrs. Kathy,

Ricky at age 3 is a little old for this behavior to be considered normal. Usually, the 18-month to 2-year-old hits, bites, and pulls hair, or all of the above. Though not to be accepted, this is the age when children develop anger and aggressive behavior.

I see that he is an only child, not yet toilet trained, and a follower. He is displaying 2-year-old behavior with the lack of impulse control for his feelings of anger and aggression. The average 2-year-old male is not toilet trained. It appears he is competing with his peers (18-month-old Robin and the 2½-year-old twins). He is the oldest in his social circle, though immature and impulsive. He needs to be taught that this negative behavior is not acceptable. You should sit down with him and his peers and discuss the rules of his society. You could tell them, "We do not push, hit, or pull hair. That hurts! If you push, pull hair, or hit, you will have to go to time-out to think about what you did and think about how to play with the other children." (Play, at this age, can also be a teaching of social skills.) Then you just send him to the time-out area for three minutes (one minute per year) with a stern "No!" He may appear to enjoy the time-out, but that is not important. The reason for time-out is to let him learn that a behavior is not acceptable; to allow him to regroup; and to re-enter his social world to try to interact positively with others. You have to be consistent with the time-out regime. Remember, discipline means to teach, not punish. By removing him from the social group for negative behavior, he will eventually learn the acceptable behavior.

By the age of 3, a child is beginning to learn to be accountable for behavior. He should be praised and rewarded for positive behavior also. The sticker chart for positive behavior is a great idea. I would suggest a shorter time frame, perhaps every half hour (possibly related to an activity) in the beginning. The attention span of a 3-year-old is only that long. The discipline technique of positive reinforcement should be tried with Ricky to reward him for positive behavior. If he is truly impulsive, he will not be able to control his behavior if not reminded of how good he is doing more often.

Chapter 4

LETTERS ON SOCIAL ISSUES

Children and Alcohol

Q

Dear Nurse Libby,

The other day Ricky, Kerrie, and Marla (all age five to six years) were playing Restaurant. Ricky was the customer, and Marla and Kerrie were the waitresses. Ricky ordered a cheeseburger and a beer. The girls looked at each other and came to me to ask what a beer was. I told Ricky that I thought he would be better with milk, and he replied, "But that's what Daddy always gets when we go to dinner." I told the girls to get him the green cup with the milk in it. With drinking such a sensitive subject for kids, how could I have handled it better? Is it okay for children to pretend that they are drinking beer?

A

Dear Mrs. Kathy,

What a powerful question! The subject of drinking alcohol and the use of drugs is something we must think about before it occurs. As you can see, the children, at four to six years, are aware of and want to mimic their parents' behavior. At this age, they are not aware of the negative consequences of overindulgence of these substances, unless they have witnessed such behavior. So, for Ricky, the beer could be just another drink, like cola or juice.

What you need to do is to find out whether Ricky or any of the other children have witnessed any negative behavior from their parents after drinking alcohol. If they seem to have not, then your matter-of-fact answer to the girls was fine and all they needed at their age. The only thing you could have added would be something like, "Ricky, I didn't know you were 21. Beer is a drink for people who are over 21 years old." If, after a discussion, you find that one of the children has witnessed the effects of overindulgence in alcohol, you could explain that sometimes some adults drink too much and it changes their behavior.

If you feel comfortable with the subject, and the children are receptive to taking in more information, you could expound on the subject. The important information to give this age group is that beer is alcohol and alcohol is for adults. Unless you gather information that makes you suspect abuse of any child, the conversation can end at this point. If you do suspect abuse, you know that by law you must report your suspicion to child protective services.

If the children were a little older, preteen, age eight or nine, you could add more information to your discussions. These children are old enough to understand that alcohol and drug use is out there. They may know an older sibling or friend who has experimented with either substance. They can understand that the use of either is against the law. They can understand that the use of either can cause their friends to act differently. They could possibly give you examples of this different behavior. Alcohol especially is very socially accepted. These preteens may be tempted to experiment with it themselves. The more information you can give them about the use and abuse of alcohol and drugs, the more you will help them.

I think the age group at the restaurant, playing grown-up, is smarter than we adults think. They watch everything we do. They may not understand the consequences of our behavior yet, but they want to be just like us. This is an outstanding example of what an important job we parents have. In all aspects of our lives, our children look up to us and expect that we take the best care of them. I hope this information is helpful to you.

Separation, Divorce, and Children

Q

Dear Nurse Libby,

Several of the children whom I watch have parents who are single. I find that it is hard for children to adjust to the fact that their parents are splitting up. Sometimes the children express concerns to me when the parents start dating. They want to know who the new person is. Will that person become the new mom or dad? I usually pass these questions along to the parents so that they are aware that their child is sensitive to what is taking place. Most often the child has not expressed these questions to the parents. I know that you went through this with your own children, and I was hoping that you could shed some personal and professional advice on this very touchy subject.

A

Dear Mrs. Kathy,

This is definitely a touchy subject. Separation, divorce, and dating are hard enough on the parent. The effects on the child are far-reaching indeed! Children experience their own type of grieving for the old familiar home they had. Even if it was a turbulent environment, the loss of the structure that provided for their support and safety—that familiar household—is mourned. Plus, they love both parents, even if their relationship was rocky.

Children will react to this issue differently, depending on their age. The preschool child will react with regressing in their developmental stage. This is displayed in sleep disturbances, fears of separation from the parent with whom they live, and irritability toward that parent and any siblings. Caregivers, other than the parent, will usually see a more easily upset and irritable child. In children five to eight years old, tears and sadness are their main reactions. They are heartbroken and sometimes feel responsible for the separation. They want more than anything for their parents to be back together. They sometimes will be extra good, hoping that if it was their fault, the parent who left will return. They are usually extra good with that parent and sometimes act out against the parent with whom they live. In preadolescents, age 9 through 12, anger is their main claim to fame during this time. They sometimes take sides with one parent, blaming the other parent. By taking sides, they also become close to one parent, sometimes too close—like a friend. The adolescent develops anger also, but it is usually accompanied with depression. They are at an increased risk for acting-out behavior such as drinking, using drugs, and increasing their sexual risky behavior. The adolescent, by nature, becomes more distant with both parents.

Add their parent dating a new person to these reactions, and you can see what will happen. The child will resent the new person, even if that person were the most perfect person in the world!

Helping parents to understand these varied reactions of children to divorce, before separating themselves, would benefit the entire family. Family counseling is VERY helpful and can sometimes save the parents' relationship. However, if the relationship is not workable after a good try at counseling, it is usually best for the parents to separate. Then, counseling can be quite effective to help the new family adjust to itself. The most favorable outcome for all is for the parents to put aside old conflicts and resume their care taking relationships with their children. As you can tell by the types of reactions of children, the younger the child, the easier the adjustment.

Now back to your original question about exposing children to the parent's new boyfriend or girlfriend too soon. This is touchy! All of us want the right relationship. We want someone we can love and who loves us for the rest of our lives. We want our soul mate! Each time we date, we hope this is the one. Sometimes, things go great for a while and then something happens. The problem is that we don't know how long "a while" is going to be. If the custodial parent has the child all the time with no breaks, it is hard to not expose the child to new friends. However, there is a way. I would advise the parents to date only when they do not have the child, for at least a couple of months into a new relationship. That means either they date when the child is with the other parent or with a baby-sitter. The parent should not have overnight dates at the home of the child during this time. This may cut down on the number of dates a parent has, but in the long run it will make for a better relationship with the child and the friend. If the friend resents this situation, the parent needs to ask, "Do I really want that kind of person in my life and around my child?" Some people need to be around other people and feel they need to be going out. I suggest counseling for all separated people—with or without children. During counseling, one can discover why they choose the type of person they do, what habits they have that maybe they want to change, and so on. In other words, we should be able to learn something about ourselves from each failed relationship. This way, hopefully we become a better person—a better parent and future partner for that soul mate!

Q

Dear Nurse Libby,

As a part of my child care, I allow the children to make special gifts for their parents for the holidays. Recently we were making something for Father's Day, and I realized that two of the children live with their mothers and their mothers' boyfriends. Because they both also have fathers who are involved in their lives, I was not sure how to handle the situation. I had only enough material for each child to make one gift.

I finally decided to let them make one gift for their father and something different for the other man in their life! Of course, all of the other children wanted to make two gifts as well, and a small project became quite an ordeal. I know that in your line of work as a pediatric nurse practitioner, you have given a lot of advice to parents. Has this topic ever come up and how would you suggest I handle this in the future?

A

Dear Mrs. Kathy,

What a lesson in sociology! It sure is a sign of the times and a great opportunity for you to teach the children about different family styles. By doing so, you can help these children be more tolerant and accepting of others who may have households different than "normal." In my almost 30 years of practice as a pediatric nurse practitioner, I have cared for patients who live in various types of households. The "normal" family can be two parents, single parents, grandparents, guardians, and other family members.

You can have a lesson on the family. Let the children explain their particular household. There may be a grandfather who lives with the child, or who is the father figure in the child's life. As you found out, it isn't always the father who has the most influence in the child's life these days. Children live with other relatives, single moms, guardians, and others. Just by discussing these differences as a normal part of their lives, the children may feel more comfortable with their "normal" family.

As far as the gifts are concerned, you have choices. These choices can get complicated. The simplest choice would be to give a gift just to the natural father (if he is involved with the child). Another choice is to let the child choose to whom to give the gift. The third choice is to give a gift to whoever is the significant male influence for each child. This choice could result in different numbers of gifts for each child to make. The children will learn that sometimes things will not always be equal. They could discuss the good things about their individual family. It hopefully would bring out positive feelings about their individual family. You may be teaching tolerance and acceptance of differences.

This also brings up the fact that children do live in diverse households. As a child care provider, this little activity brings out the importance of you knowing the social environment of your children. For special crafts and activities involving specific family members, you should consult with the guardian/parent of each child to be sure you are knowledgeable about their individual situations. Therefore, a Father's Day gift could become a grandfather/uncle gift.

Q

Dear Nurse Libby,

Casey's (age four) parents have recently separated, and I have noticed that she has been making up these unusual songs. She will sit on the porch alone and sing about being lost in the woods and that she is dying and crying. I realize that she is acting out. What should I do or say to help her through this difficult time? I told her mother about this incident, and she was truly alarmed.

A

Dear Mrs. Kathy,

I will try to help. By you telling her mother and her mother's reaction, hopefully Casey will get the help she needs. Separation of parents obviously affects everyone in the household. Sometimes, children are put in the middle. What I mean by this is that the parent will talk with the child about the other parent, will not allow the child to see the other parent as a punishment to that parent, and even get the child to spy on the other parent.

The age of the child also affects their reaction. Obviously, an infant and even young toddler is less affected because they don't understand all the emotional impact yet. They can adjust to new caregivers, as long as there is stability and routines in their lives. By the age of three, most children have memories. So, when one parent is no longer there, and stability and routine are disrupted, they will react. At four years of age, Casey has a memory and an imagination. If you remember, this is the age of nightmares and imaginary friends. So, Casey's reaction by making up these sad songs is actually healthy grieving. Her parents need to reassure her that each of them is still there for her. Hopefully, they will develop a routine that puts stability in Casey's life, which includes both of them. If this is done, then Casey will adjust and start singing happy songs again! Obviously, because of all the emotions of divorce, this is easier said than done. So, your role in this situation would be to monitor Casey's progress during the transition in her life and see whether she returns to a happy little four-year-old.

As children get older, the separation of their parents affects them more. This should be obvious, but it is not to a lot of people. Parents need to realize that their child is hurting also. Children always, no matter how old they get (even as mature adults), subconsciously want their parents to stay together. Due to developmental stages, early school age children are usually the least dramatic in their reactions. They still grieve, but they adjust more easily. Adolescents will react more. Just think about it, they are going through all the regular upheavals of adolescence and then a separation of their parents occurs! How could these parents do this to them? That is how adolescents think. The child who has the toughest time adjusting is the older (14 and older) adolescent male. He is starting to date himself; this is his time (so to speak). To see his parents dating and partying, especially the mother, is extremely difficult for him. Sometimes, counseling is necessary and very helpful during this time. I hope this information is helpful not only for the four-year-old, but for all children who have to face the separation of their parents.

Bonding

Q

Dear Nurse Libby,

One of the reasons that I became a child care provider is because I felt that I missed so much of my daughter's childhood because I went to work each day. As I stay home now, I realize that there is nothing stronger then a bond between a parent and child. Yes, sometimes it seems that I am with the child more than the parents are. I do experience that first step or the first word that a child might speak, but a child will always love his or her mother and father in a powerful special way, one that I cannot replace.

In the past some of the babies have referred to me as mommy. I always correct the child and explain that I am not mommy, but that I am mommy's helper when she is away. I know the pain a mother feels when she hears this, for I have had this happen to me with my daughter. I just had to tell myself that I was happy that my child was comfortable with the child care provider and remember that this too shall pass. What is your feeling on this delicate subject?

A

Dear Mrs. Kathy,

These are words of wisdom with compassion. Your children and parents sure are lucky to have you for a child care provider! These thoughts, hopefully, are reassuring to the parents. It is hard to go to work everyday and leave your child in the hands of someone else. Children are our most important possession and our future. The bond between a parent and child is unbreakable.

Parents who are comfortable with their child care provider or teacher realize that they are a team in molding the future of their children. I hope by revealing these feelings, we can help ensure that most children who are in any form of child care are cared for by compassionate and understanding people.

Nail Biting

Q

Dear Nurse Libby,

Robin (age two years) has been chewing her fingernails, to the point that they are bleeding and covered in sores. As you may remember from a prior letter, she is the one that was chewing my wicker chair! Do you think she just has a habit of chewing, or could there be a problem?

A

Dear Mrs. Kathy,

Two-year-olds usually do not chew their fingernails. Nail biting is usually a sign of stress. A two-year-old usually does not experience stress, but can pick up on the stress of others. If her parents are not upset about anything and neither of them has the same habit, she should be evaluated by a primary care provider. How is she when they come to get her? I think there is something going on with Robin. I would need more information to help you. The person who really needs the help is Robin. Her parents need to discuss this with her primary care provider, especially if the chewing is as severe as you describe. Hopefully, her parents will take this seriously. At the least, Robin could experience severe bacterial infections from the chewing.

Last Day at Child Care

Q

Dear Nurse Libby,

Samantha (age 15 months) will be leaving my child care to move out of state. As you may recall, her mother is pregnant with twins and Samantha had experienced separation anxiety. On your advice, her mother had her evaluated by her primary care provider and was told that Samantha is a very sensitive child. Samantha's mother cut back her hours at work so that she could spend more time with Samantha. It became very obvious that this time spent together has eased Samantha's separation anxiety.

I am truly happy for all the positive things going on with Samantha and her family. However, I feel like I am losing my own child. This will be a very hard day for me. I am not sure how to handle this situation to make it easy on the other child care kids, Samantha, her family, and me. Should I have a party to say good-bye, or just let the day end like all others?

A

Dear Mrs. Kathy,

This should be a hard day for you! You are letting go of a piece of your heart! These are good feelings, though. They are a display of the type of caring child care provider you are. Anyone who has a child in child care should be lucky to have someone who feels these emotions at a time like this.

To answer your question, though, yes, by all means have a party! Let the children help in the preparation. It is good for them to help in preparing them to say good-bye to someone with whom they have spent a year. Samantha will be the center of attention for the last day with you, so you can enjoy your last day together. Her mother will leave with more reassurance that Samantha has spent her first formative year in a caring environment. This is a great way for everyone to feel good about the year spent together, as well as celebrate Samantha and her family's new move. Hope you have a great day!

There will be some tears of good-bye. However, remember, that you played an important part in getting Samantha where she is today. The tears can then be tears of joy!

Sensitivity to Our Differences

Q

Dear Nurse Libby,

The other day, during our lesson, I went around the room and I asked each child what they thought made them different or special from everyone else in the room. The one twin stated that she was different because she was a twin, the other twin pointed out that she had red hair. Marla pointed out that she was the only one in the room without a brother or sister. When it was Antoine's (age eight) turn to comment, one of the children pointed out that he was different because he was black. I could tell that this embarrassed him. I immediately responded that yes his skin color was a different color. When I went back to him and asked him the question again, he said that he did not want to play. How could I have handled this situation differently?

A

Dear Mrs. Kathy,

Children can surely be insensitive!! The good thing is that most children, up through early school age, don't realize they are being insensitive. I am assuming that Antoine is the only African American in your child care. The same scenario probably would have happened if the racial difference were the opposite, with the white child being described as being different by skin color. Young children see things mostly in likes and differences that are concrete, like skin color. All of the children's examples of how they were different were things they could see, not things they could feel. No one gave a talent, such as the best at coloring, as a reason for being different.

I do have a few thoughts on how you could have handled the situation differently. Now, knowing how children think at this age, you could have simply told the child who pointed out the skin color that is was not his turn to speak. You had asked the question to Antoine, not anyone else. If you had said this in that matter-of-fact manner, the focus of the conversation may have reverted back to what you had intended.

Another idea would be to acknowledge the difference the other child pointed out, with no explanation, and proceed to ask Antoine what he thought was different about himself. Maybe, with no elaboration on the skin color, Antoine would not have felt as different as he appeared to feel after your discussion.

Because you did discuss skin color, you could have looked at the subtle different shades of each of the other children's skin tones and discussed these as differences also. This discussion would possibly have downplayed skin tone differences altogether for this age group.

However, racial difference is a reality. Simply stating the skin color difference as you did, and trying to get the game started again, could have been the best way to manage the situation also. Children, at this age, are resilient. They all, including Antoine, have probably gone past this conversation and are equal as friends at your child care.

Q

Dear Nurse Libby:

As a follow-up to the question on sensitivity to our differences, I think I was more sensitive about the issue than the children were. I was afraid that Antoine was embarrassed or hurt by the comment, because he did not want to continue playing the game. However, the next day over breakfast, the older kids started the game again. Antoine was one of the first to comment about how good he was at drawing cartoons.

You were right. Children at this age are resilient.

Death and Dying

Q

Dear Nurse Libby,

The other day, I reminded the children (age four and five) not to give the dogs "people food" because it would make them sick. They responded to my comment by saying, "That's right Mrs. Kathy, and they could die." Marla (age five) commented, "Well, if they die we will never see them again, right?" I agreed with her, and the conversation ended there. But it made me stop and think. How much do children understand about death and dying? At what age should we adults discuss it with them? What do we tell them?

A

Dear Mrs. Kathy,

Out of the mouths of babes comes so much wisdom. Your short conversation with the four- and five-year-olds displays beautifully how much they understand about death and dying. The fact that they just stated their facts and did not get into emotions shows that they deal with death in a matter of fact manner. Before the age of eight years, most children do not fully understand the permanency of death. Although, if they are exposed to someone who is terminally ill and in the stages of dying, they will experience a sense of danger and doom. They will pick up sad, possibly anxious feelings from parents and other people close to them and involved with the person who is dying. They may or may not act on these feelings. Most young children react only when the death actually occurs.

In an ideal world, we as adults should try to foresee things that our children will be exposed to and either protect them from or prepare them for it. Most of us try to accomplish this in most things children have to face, like going to school, a new house, and other new experiences. The subject of death seems to rarely come up. Yet it is a part of everyone's life. Our children will be exposed to it. We caregivers should take the opportunities in nature as they arise to discuss death with our children. If a cat kills a bird and the dead bird is in the yard, instead of sweeping the bird off to the trash quickly, we can use it to show that all living creatures die. Young children will at least see what death looks like at this point. The still bird that looks like it is sleeping can be their first exposure. If a distant relative dies, discuss that they will never see the person again. This helps them to understand the finality of death. However, don't expect children under the age of eight to comprehend the full impact of death. They may ask again where the person or pet went. We need to be understanding and sensitive to each child's level of comprehension. After the exposure is given, answer only the exact question being asked. After the age of eight, children are able to assimilate the full impact of death being final.

If a child has to experience the death of a loved one, I recommend counseling for the entire family, to help everyone understand the child's perspective. In what follows, I have taken the liberty to include some suggestions to help a child through grief.

Suggestions to Help a Child through Grief

Remember to

- Not underestimate the child's grief.
- Let the child feel her pain and loss her way.
- Realize that the child may not respond to loss in the same way you might. Some may cry, and some may not cry.

- Let the child express grief physically—maybe beat a soft object, pound on something, or just run the feelings out.
- Allow the child to talk about his grief in his own manner. He will tell you how he feels in his words or in his behavior.
- Talk about the person (or pet) who died with the child. She will want to talk sometimes and sometimes not. Let the child be the guide, but do not be afraid to bring up the deceased in conversation.
- Avoid statements like "Now you're the man of the house." This would allow the child to assume the role of emotional caregiver to his parents.
- Not worry about the child's appetite. If she is not eating much, she will return to normal. Just give plenty of fluids.
- Give the child plenty of time to grieve. He may feel the loss and express it for a long time.
- Speak the truth about the death. Children are concrete thinkers. As an example, instead of saying, "Grandpa passed away," say, "Grandpa died."
- Discuss death honestly. If the child asks whether you will die, be honest. You can say, "I think I will live until I'm very old, but no one knows for sure."
- Treat the child as normal as possible. Avoid singling him out for special privileges. He needs to feel he is treated the same as the other children.
- Continue the same structure, rules, and limits the child had before the grief occurred. It provides security.
- Tell the truth ("I don't know" is an appropriate answer to "Why" questions).
- Touch, hold, or hug the child when appropriate.
- Talk about loss and death before a significant death occurs, if possible. Visit a cemetery; use nature (e.g., dead bird) for discussion.
- Tell the child that she did not cause the death by her angry thoughts.
- Allow the child to select the play activities he needs to work through his grief.
- Let the child "talk" about her feelings through drawings.
- Give the child something to do—for example, write a story. It will combat her helplessness.
- Read children's books that deal with loss so that the child knows that his feelings are normal.
- Use third-person language when talking to children. It is less threatening. Say, "Many children feel," instead of "Do YOU feel?"
- Talk about the loss WHENEVER the child brings up the subject.
- Answer only what is asked. Let the child be in charge of what she is ready to hear.
- Expect children to regress somewhat—that is, to cling, be afraid, want to be rocked to sleep, and have night-lights on.
- Tell the child the exact cause of death ("Grandma's heart wouldn't work anymore").

I hope this overview helps you in answering these critically important and confusing questions!

Chapter 5

LETTERS ON SLEEP

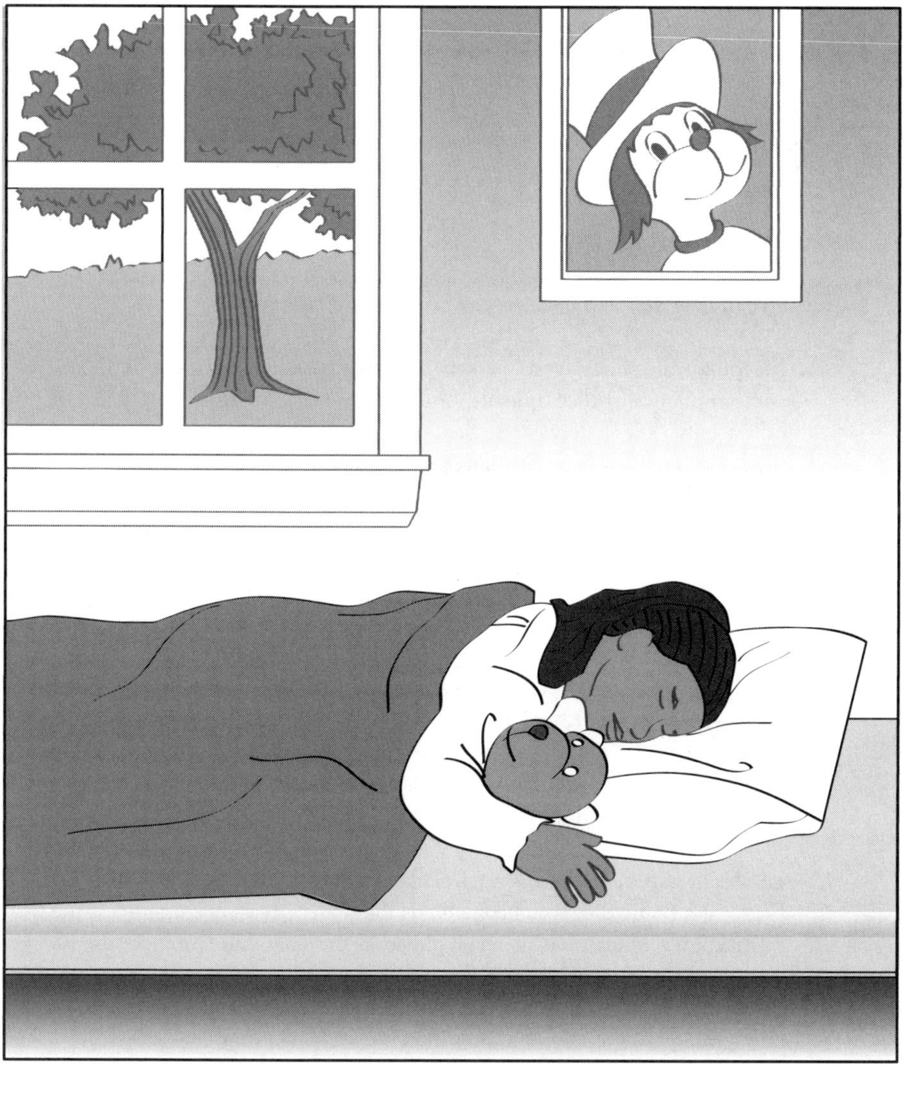

Security Blanket

Q

Dear Nurse Libby,

I have never been one to clutter a crib with pillows, blankets, and stuffed animals. At what age do you suggest children sleep with pillows and blankets? What is your opinion on stuffed animals? What about bottles at nap time?

A

Dear Mrs. Kathy,

I will try to help you and give you my opinion and concerns.

1. Sleeping with pillows and blankets. All infants should sleep flat on their back with no pillows, stuffed animals, or loose blankets. Children should not be given a pillow until they no longer use the crib. Their airway is not developed enough for the neck to be bent any. Sleeping without a pillow is also great for children who snore! By lying flat, the airway is extended, and children are less likely to snore, which is usually caused from enlarged tonsils and adenoids. Blankets are okay after one year old. I guess you are referring to the security blanket.

2. Stuffed animals. These are okay after the age of one year also. The problem with stuffed animals is the removable parts—eyes and nose especially. A child can spend time biting and pulling these removable parts off and either eating them or putting them in other body cavities they have. Ears and nose are common sites. Choking on a button eye or getting pneumonia from a foreign body (a button eye) happens too much. Make sure there are no removable parts, even if you have to remove them yourself!

3. Bottles at nap time. This is a particular issue with me! A baby should NEVER be given a bottle unless someone holds the bottle! The sucking urge is the first satisfaction a human has. Being cuddled at the same time promotes bonding and emotional satisfaction—that is, love! Putting a baby down anywhere with the bottle is wrong. After the age of 15 months, the toddler should be off the bottle! It only promotes dental cavities after that age. The sucking urge may still be there,

though. That is why I recommend a pacifier. Pacifiers do not cause cavities or choking and can be thrown away when the sucking urge stage is over. This stage may last until the child is 2 to 2½ years old. Before nap time, give the toddler a drink out of a cup and give the pacifier, if needed. If the bottle is taken away and the pacifier has not been introduced, and the sucking urge is still present, the child will resort to his thumb, which CANNOT be thrown away!

I hope these answers help!

Nap Time, Quiet Time

Q

Dear Nurse Libby,

I normally have the children take a rest period between noon and 2:00 P.M. I have a child who is four years old and his mother does not want him to sleep during the day because she puts him to bed at 7:00 P.M. I have suggested to her that he can lie down and rest, but he always seems to fall asleep. She would like him to be permitted to play in a different section of the nap area so that I see him and the other children at the same time. When I tried this, all the other children complained because he was allowed to play and they had to sleep. It seems to me that if he is falling asleep, then he needs the rest. What is your suggestion?

A

Dear Mrs. Kathy,

Most child care businesses have structure to help set up the day. If one child is allowed to not follow the rules, this sends him or her and the other children a message. The special child gets a message that they do not have to follow the rules set up for the rest. The other children get a message that maybe they do not have to follow rules either, and/or they may resent the child who does not follow the rules.

Usually a four-year-old still requires a nap. The fact that he falls asleep supports that. By the age of six or seven years, the child may just require quiet time. You could offer that age group books or small puzzles to occupy them while they rest.

A child care center has to have structure in the day. Most centers, even those larger than yours, have a nap time. This nap/quiet time is for everyone. To allow for a structured child care to run an organized center, all the children must be on the same schedule. Maybe you could have a list of the rules of your child care center. These could be given to any prospective parent. They could then see how you run the business, not only for nap time but also for activity time, lesson time, and free play. The parents, I think, would feel reassured that the children are not just watched but allowed to grow developmentally under your care.

Q

Dear Nurse Libby,

Nap time can sometimes be a difficult transition for some children. My child care children are usually worn out and are ready to rest by noon. Most of the children have to wake up at 6:30 in the morning as well. On occasion I will have a child who will not nap. The child will cry and become very upset. I have the children who are in cribs sleep in rooms alone. The older children all sleep together on separate mats. I check on the children every 15 minutes to make sure they are safe and sleeping. My question is how long should I allow someone to cry at nap time?

A

Dear Mrs. Kathy,

As you already stated, most children will fall asleep without problems. So whatever routine you are following is working. Usually what is recommended for sleep problems is to put the child down for the nap and leave. Do this with a watch with a second hand visible! After one minute of the child crying, go in and put the child down for the nap and leave. After two minutes of the child crying, go in and put the child down for the nap and leave. After three minutes, four minutes, and so on, repeat the process. Each time, and especially if there are other children in the room, do not talk to the child. Just give them physical contact to gently lay them down for naptime and leave. It may take up to 20 to 30 minutes for the child to fall asleep (worst case). Usually, this method works within two weeks. Consistency and structure in a happy loving manner is the best caregiving any child can have. I know that is what you give them.

Q

Dear Nurse Libby,

Robin (age two years) has started to scream when I put her down for a nap. I know that she is tired because she is almost falling asleep in her lunch. She has been off the pacifier for 6 months, and she has been bringing a special doll to sleep with. I discussed this concern with her mom, and she said that Robin has been doing the same thing at bedtime. I noticed that she has teeth coming in in the back, could this be the problem? How should I handle this situation?

A

Dear Mrs. Kathy,

How long has the screaming at naptime been going on? If it is since she has stopped taking the pacifier, this could be easy. Was it her decision to stop the pacifier? If the answer to the previous two questions is Yes and No, respectfully, then give her the pacifier back. The fact that she is doing the same thing at bedtime at home makes me think she was forced to give up the pacifier. The sucking urge can continue past the second birthday. It varies with each child. If she used the pacifier just to fall asleep, she may not be at the stage yet to fall asleep by herself. Having a special doll to sleep with is another clue that it was not her decision to give up the pacifier. As long as she only had the pacifier to fall asleep, and not hanging around her neck all the time, she probably needs the sucking to settle herself to sleep. It is normal to need the sucking urge, for this purpose, past the second birthday.

Teething her molars may make her more irritable, but the irritability should be prevalent throughout the day and not just at nap or bedtime. In compliance with your state rules and regulations, you can give her the proper dose of acetaminophen or ibuprofen for the pain. It may help her.

Q

Dear Nurse Libby,

I wanted to get back to you about Robin screaming at nap time. I asked her mother if she had the same situation at home and she said yes. At that point she told me that she started letting Robin sleep in bed with her. My sense is that Robin is screaming now because she does not want to sleep alone.

A

Dear Mrs. Kathy,

Robin probably does not want to sleep alone. During the day, at the child care center, you must continue the routine you have established. Therefore, Robin will have to cry (scream) herself to sleep. Use a watch with a second hand, as described previously. Usually, if you continue your routine and not give in to her, she will eventually (hopefully sooner than later) settle into the routine.

Q

Dear Nurse Libby,

Several of my parents have brought their babies into my child care in those little carrying chairs and have asked me to let the children sleep in the chair for a nap. The babies seem to sleep well in these chairs, but I'm wondering if this is safe and healthy for the baby. At what age should I stop allowing them to sleep in the chair?

A

Dear Mrs. Kathy,

It is okay to allow an infant to sleep in the little infant chair. These chairs are most often very sturdy structurally and well padded for comfort. They are designed for the anatomical body of an infant. So I think you are safe in using them for the infant from birth to four to six months old. Infancy usually refers to the first year of life. By the time the infant is four to six months old, most of them can sit alone! Some still need a little support, but the infant can pull forward and attempt to sit alone by this age. Once the child is attempting to sit alone or is already doing so, the infant seat is too small for the child to be left unattended, awake or asleep!

A lot of infants are diagnosed with reflux. This is a condition where the infant spits up after feedings repeatedly. The cause is thought to be an immature esophagus (the tube that goes from the mouth to the stomach). The food goes down okay, but due to the constant contracting of the esophagus, the food comes back up. Keeping the child sitting up after feedings helps this condition. Because most young infants eat every three to four hours, they are usually kept sitting up between feeds, thus sleeping in their infant seat. As luck would have it, this condition usually resolves on its own between the ages of six months and one year. This is the same time frame that the infant is able to sit alone with no support, is standing and possibly walking, and is eating solid foods. It is the same time frame that the infant is getting too active to be left in the infant chair unattended. As an aside, if you have an infant who vomits (forceful regurgitation, food goes across the room), this would not be reflux. This infant eats the same, is happy, but then the food comes back forcefully AND the child doesn't seem to be gaining weight. This could be pyloric stenosis, a blockage of the opening of the stomach into the intestine. This condition has to be surgically repaired. It usually occurs in first-born male babies.

Another, very important reason for having the infant sleep in the infant chair is to prevent SIDS, sudden infant death syndrome. Studies have been done to show that the infant who sleeps on her back has a much lesser chance of succumbing to SIDS. The infant chair is positioned so that the infant sleeps on her back, obviously. This is probably the main reason that a lot of your mothers are asking you to allow their infants to sleep in the infant chair. Coincidentally, again, the age at which one can relax about the possibility of SIDS occurring is six months.

Q

Dear Nurse Libby,

One of the things that fascinates my parents the most is that I can get eight children to lie down and take a nap at the same time every day. Parents express to me the difficulty that they experience trying to put the children down at night and also dealing with them when they wake up in the middle of the night. When I put the children down for naps, they realize that it is time to be quite and rest. I have had some difficulty in the beginning with the new children, but after a few days they get the hang of it. Can you provide me with some suggestions that I can pass along to the parents to make going to bed and staying in bed a success?

A

Dear Mrs. Kathy,

First I would like to address the difference between nap time and bedtime. I assume that the children you are discussing, with the sleep problems at home, are mostly preschoolers who do still need and take a nap. Most of these children are probably awakened early in the morning to allow the parents time to get to your house and then to work on time. So by nap time they are tired. They are also usually not alone in the nap room, and it is not dark out. There is also consistency in the time they arise in the morning and the time they are to lie down for their nap. That is why it only takes a new child a few days to get with the schedule. Nap time, as the name implies, is for a much shorter time then bedtime. The child arises after only one to three hours. Even at that, I'm sure you have some preschoolers who do not actually fall asleep, as they no longer physically require sleep during the day. Although, a good nap never hurts anyone!

Now for bedtime, sleeping problems are a different matter altogether! These problems are different, partially, due to the length of time one is supposed to sleep. Normal sleep is made up of two cycling different states. The rapid eye movement (REM) state is the very active state both mentally and physically. One goes into deep sleep and light sleep during this state, which lasts approximately in 1½ hour cycles. Dreams occur during this state, and the sleeper can be restless and move around. Most of the dreaming and restlessness occur during the second half of the night.

Non–rapid-eye-movement (NREM) sleep is the other cycling state. This state is what we think of as sleep. To get to this state, the child goes through four stages. Light sleep is the first, which involves reduced body movements and eye rolling. Stage 2 occurs as the eye movements slow and breathing slows to an even rhythm. Stages 3 and 4 are very similar and are the deepest NREM stages where the body is totally relaxed. Nighttime sleep consists of these two states repeatedly alternating.

The NREM state is the first stage one goes through to get to sleep, with the deepest NREM sleep occurring during the first one to three hours after going to sleep. It is important to understand these states, as dreaming and nightmares occur during the REM stage.

Many children have sleep problems. Most of the problems are related to irregular sleep habits or fear of going to sleep in the dark. The first irregular sleep habit occurs around six to nine months of age. The baby is going through separation anxiety, is learning to think and recognize people, and is learning to dream. These dreams wake him up and he cries. What most parents think is that the baby is hungry, and so they feed him. He learns this habit and repeats the episodes every night. Along with everyone's sleep being broken up nightly, no infant after six months of age needs to be fed in the middle of the night. But, what to do with the crying baby? Go into the room when he cries and give him a pacifier. Sucking is still the strongest urge at this time, and he will suck himself back to sleep. Do not turn on lights, pick him up, or talk. If you do this routine, the baby will learn that sucking the pacifier allows him to return to sleep. You may have to return to the room every few minutes for a few nights. The infant will learn the behavior if you are consistent and don't give in to talking to him or cuddling him. We would all like to be cuddled all night! One of my own sons would actually find the pacifier himself in the crib and put it in his mouth.

A lot of sleep problems are associated with irregular sleep habits. The bedtime ritual is very important. If the child perceives sleep as a normal part of their daily schedule and the time is consistent, with their age, then going to bed will be easier. Consistent and regular sleep routines, as you have for nap time, will resolve most common sleep problems.

When all of these fail, it usually means you have a child who is going through the nightmare stage. This stage usually occurs around the age of four to six years. Sometimes daytime stresses can cause nightmares. Television programs that are too violent for the four-year-old are a big cause. If there are any stressful changes going on in the family or in child care, the child can react with nightmares. As with the infant, you are going to have to go into the child's room. She is old enough to talk to, so reassure her that everything is okay. Leaving a night-light on helps this age group, especially if they are afraid to go to sleep. The parent may have to stay with the child until she falls back to sleep, reassuring her that she is safe. The parent should investigate family and daytime stresses and eliminate them if possible. If one is consistent with the ritual at bedtime and during the awakenings, this too shall pass!

There are some nighttime awakenings that are more severe. Night terrors are the most common and are sometimes accompanied by sleepwalking. These problems occur during the first two hours after falling asleep and only affect about 3 percent of children. These children will sit up in bed, scream and thrash about, incoherently. They are essentially not awake! They are not comforted by parents. This is scary for the parent. The attack can last a few minutes to a half hour. The child then goes back to normal sleep and has no memory of the event. If any parents describe such an event to you, have them discuss it with their primary care provider. Treatment is available. The good news is that as children mature, they usually get over sleep problems, even the severe ones!

Chapter 6

LETTERS ON EATING HABITS

Meals and Schedules

Q

Dear Nurse Libby,

I have several questions on children and eating and I hope you can give me some guidance. I do provide all the meals at my home, and I have included a menu to assist in answering my questions.

7:00–8:00	BREAKFAST:	For example: pancakes, fruit, milk
9:30–10:00	SNACK:	For example: crackers, peanut butter, raisins, milk
11:30–12:00	LUNCH:	For example: chicken strips, fries, green beans, bread, milk
3:00–3:30	SNACK:	For example: soft pretzel, cheese, milk

1. *Should children be permitted to have a snack if they do not finish their meal?*
2. *Should children be forced to clean their plate?*
3. *If the child does not like what is being served, should I make her something different?*
4. *Should I limit the amount of food a child is permitted to eat?*
5. *Is there such a thing as too much milk?*
6. *I provide water throughout the day for the children. One of my parents wanted me to make her three-year-old drink a glass of water before meals so that she would not eat as much at lunchtime. The child was eating the same portions as the other children. She appears to be of average height and weight to me.*

A

Dear Mrs. Kathy,

You sure do have some questions! I guess I'll just take your questions in order. Again, what is right for one household may not be right for another. As long as the basics are correct, sometimes both sides of an issue are correct. Now that I have confused you even more, let me tackle these issues on food.

1. The snack without finishing the meal. From the example you have provided, your snack can almost be a meal. Children vary in their appetites. Age, growth spurts, and activity level all play a part. Some children may not like to eat early in the morning, just like some adults claim that they are not breakfast people. Toddlers, after they have tripled their birth weight (which happens around one year of age), have a small appetite. If they eat ONE good meal a day, feel lucky! School-age children usually have appetites that come and go, coincidentally with their growth spurts. So if parents and caregivers offer good nutritious foods and no real junk food, and let the child pick from the offerings, the child will get what is needed. To specifically answer your question, I agree with you to allow the child to skip a meal and eat a snack as long as the snack is a good nutritious food source.

2. Cleaning the plate. Mealtimes with children can be fun or a chore. Because of reasons already discussed in question 1, children between the ages of 1 and about 12 years go through phases with their appetites. They still need to be exposed to different and nutritious foods. A rule of thumb, which works and takes the chore out of mealtime, is this: Have the child try a new vegetable, with this being the rule for all meals. They have to eat ever how many years old they are in bites! So, the three-year-old must eat three bites of peas! Now the bite can be a half a spoonful or what can be picked up with a fork! This being the rule, the child knows what is expected at dinner. The other issue with cleaning the plate is portion sizes. Start out with a small tablespoon size for beginning portions. The child may surprise you, and ask for seconds!

3. Child likes and dislikes. State-run child care centers usually offer various choices of meals, or they require a bag lunch. The children can pick what they want for lunch. Home child care menus can be state regulated if you participate in the food program. Menus are usually more limited in choices, so again a parent may wish to provide a bag lunch. The important thing is to offer nutritious choices. Using the rule from question 2, the child should eat the appropriate portion of the food in question. Even if he has already tried it and knows he doesn't like it, this should be the rule. The reason for this is because as children grow, they

develop new taste buds, so the child who doesn't like broccoli today may indeed love it tomorrow!

4. The big eater. The key word in your question is SOMETIMES! Occasionally, and during growth spurts, a child may appear to gorge himself. He will eat anything and all of it! He usually quits when he is full. Again, as long as the diet is balanced with the offerings being good nutritious food, let the child be the guide. The other consideration for the big eater, though, is body size. If the child were indeed overweight, then you would have to limit his choices and portions. This should only be done under the guidance of a nutritionist or primary care provider.

5. Milk amounts. I will start at birth and explain the milk needs. The infant, birth to one year of age, requires an iron-fortified formula in the amounts of 26 to 40 ounces a day (depending on the amount of solid food they are eating). After one year of age, most toddlers can have whole milk. The required amount drops to about 8 to 10 ounces a day! The reason the amount is so low is simple. Think about it. They are not growing at the rapid rate they did during their first year of life. They just tripled their birth weight! They can't keep that up for too long, so body needs naturally drop off. So if toddlers drink too much milk, they will eat very little food. Some toddlers become anemic (low levels of iron) by drinking too much milk. They must be given whole milk until they reach the age of two. Then anyone can have skim milk. After the age of two, the milk amounts vary according to those growth spurts I've already mentioned. The average amount of milk is 4 to 6 ounces, one to three times a day. Remember, they get other dairy products throughout the day. As the child approaches adolescence, the milk intake increases dramatically. Think about all that bone mass development! Some parents may want to buy a cow! I guess to answer your question, yes, at different growth times, there is such a thing as too much milk.

6. Water before meals. I would have to know more about this particular situation. If the child is indeed overweight and under the care of a nutritionist or primary care provider, you should follow the diet outlined for this child. For an adult, drinking a glass of water prior to a meal is helpful. We are not growing. For a child, I would need to know the percentile of weight and height to comment. However, water is good for an older child who is approaching adolescence. Three-year-olds need a good nutritious diet balanced with activity (physical exercise) to maintain a healthy body weight for their respective height. Water is a good part of this diet for anyone over the age of six months and should be offered throughout the day.

Q

Dear Nurse Libby,

I know that we have discussed children and eating in the past, but I am concerned about Josh (age five years). He is a very picky eater and does not like any form of pasta or meat. He would, however, eat hot dogs and peanut butter and jelly every day.

This puts me in a difficult situation for several reasons. The first problem with making him what he wants is that everyone else will want it. If I do not make him a hot dog or peanut butter and jelly sandwich, he will go to school on an empty stomach. He will, however, eat the fruits and vegetables that I serve with lunch. Is it healthy for him to skip the protein and carbohydrates and eat just fruit and vegetables? Sometimes I will put a scoop of peanut butter on his fruit just to get protein in him. I have tried in the past to explain to the other children that I make different things for Josh because he does not like what we are having. This raises problems when I serve something that one of the other children does not like and I tell that child to try and eat it. The other children want to know why Josh gets special things to eat but they do not. I do not make any of them clean their plate, but before they get seconds on something, they need to eat what is already on their plate. I also will give someone a small portion of a food that I know he or she does not like so he or she does not have to struggle with it. What do you think?

A

Dear Mrs. Kathy,

Children do vary in their appetites. They are not all having growth spurts at the same time either. They also come to your child care center from different families—each family having their own likes and dislikes about food. Some adults, as well as some children, are not traditional breakfast food eaters. With all these variables, I can understand your dilemma with meal preparation. You do need to provide healthy meals for the children. I'm sure there are guidelines for meals in your state rules and regulations for child care centers by which you must abide also.

If you can provide limited nutritional choices for meals and allow all the children to pick from the choices, then everyone will be happy. The choices could be posted, as menus, for parents to see and possibly discuss with the child before each day. If you are limited to one choice per meal, that too could be posted for parent and child to review. Then, if the child did not like the choice for the day, maybe the parent could provide a meal for that day. This recommendation would eliminate the problem of Josh getting special things to eat and prevent him from going to school hungry. Breakfast is the most important meal of the day for children and adults. Even if he doesn't eat a traditional breakfast food, he needs to eat something. Hot dogs and peanut butter and jelly sandwiches are both good sources of protein and carbohydrates for proper brain function.

Your idea of using small portions for foods you know someone does not like is a good one. I suggest you use small portions for all foods, and give seconds to those who want them. This way, you can be more certain that the balanced meal you are serving is eaten. As long as what you offer the children is good nutritious food, let them pick what they want. Sometimes the growing body of one child needs more protein for muscle growth, whereas another child needs more carbohydrates for energy. So if Josh skips the protein and eats the fruits and vegetables, that is what he needs at the time.

Children require different nutrients at different times in growing years. An infant who triples birth weight from birth to age one requires more nutrients than a preschooler. A three-year-old's growth pattern is slower. She grows in slower increments, therefore actually requiring fewer nutrients. Imagine, if she continued to triple her weight every year. A teenage boy will eat and drink most anything in the house during his growth spurts. He needs a lot of protein and calcium for muscle mass and long bone growth. I will include here a copy of the food pyramid, which categorizes food sources and amounts for different age groups. I hope this information will help your meal preparation dilemma.

FOOD Guide PYRAMID

for Young Children

A Daily Guide for 2- to 6-Year-Olds

U.S. Department of Agriculture
Center for Nutrition Policy and Promotion

January 2000
Program Aid 1651

USDA is an equal opportunity provider and employer.

FOOD IS FUN and learning about food is fun, too. Eating foods from the Food Guide Pyramid and being physically active will help you grow healthy and strong.

WHAT COUNTS AS ONE SERVING?

GRAIN GROUP
1 slice of bread
½ cup of cooked rice or pasta
½ cup of cooked cereal
1 ounce of ready-to-eat cereal

VEGETABLE GROUP
½ cup of chopped raw
or cooked vegetables
1 cup of raw leafy vegetables

FRUIT GROUP
1 piece of fruit or melon wedge
¾ cup of juice
½ cup of canned fruit
¼ cup of dried fruit

MILK GROUP
1 cup of milk or yogurt
2 ounces of cheese

MEAT GROUP
2 to 3 ounces of cooked lean meat, poultry, or fish.

½ cup of cooked dry beans, or 1 egg counts as 1 ounce of lean meat. 2 tablespoons of peanut butter count as 1 ounce of meat.

FATS AND SWEETS
Limit calories from these.

Four- to 6-year-olds can eat these serving sizes. Offer 2- to 3-year-olds less, except for milk. Two- to 6-year-old children need a total of 2 servings from the milk group each day.

EAT a variety of FOODS AND ENJOY!

Source: U.S. Department of Agriculture

Chewing Development

Q

Dear Nurse Libby,

Andy, who is now turning one, has a difficult time eating "people food". I started him on crackers and dry cereal and he gags on them. He now has seven teeth in the front. What would you suggest for his diet?

A

Dear Mrs. Kathy,

Some children are slower developing the ability to chew than others. This is another developmental milestone (as we have labeled them). Offer him things that are softer than crackers and dry cereal. Try applesauce, yogurt with fruit, bananas, and vegetable soup (small, soft vegetables; omit any corn), or a scrambled egg. If he has difficulty with any of the above foods, just omit that particular food for a while. You can reintroduce any difficult food substance every couple of months. His chewing will most likely develop by the age of two years.

How does he do drinking from a cup? If by the age of two, he is still choking on most things, and/or he is not able to drink from a cup, he needs to be evaluated by his primary care provider.

Weight Issues

Q

Dear Nurse Libby,

Recently one of my nine-year-old girls got off the bus complaining that the kids were teasing her because she is fat. To me this child looks to be a normal weight. I asked her what she weighs and how tall she was and she told me she is 78 pounds and 53 inches tall. She told me she wears a size 10 in pants. What do you tell a child to encourage good eating habits and not to worry about dieting?

A

Dear Mrs. Kathy,

A lot of preadolescents go through a fat phase. No two preadolescents grow and gain weight exactly the same. Kids don't always understand that and can be cruel. As long as the child is eating a good nutritious diet—not a lot of junk food—she will probably be fine. We are, however, raising a lot of obese children. They eat mostly a fast food type of diet. This diet is high in fat and carbohydrates. The children are not getting enough fruit and vegetables in their diet on a regular basis.

The other piece of the puzzle is exercise. Preadolescents are in an awkward place here also. They are getting too old to play running games with their peers; they start to get into the telephone and/or the computer. A lot of them are in no organized sport.

So what to tell this young lady? First, reassure her that she is not finished growing yet and that people do not grow and gain weight at the same pace. Next, encourage her to start participating in her diet. Make sure she knows about good nutritious foods so that she can evaluate her diet. Advise her to exercise regularly. Include her parents in on the discussion, if possible.

The media has done a great job with projecting that thin is attractive, and most of our children watch the media. Children seem to be maturing at an earlier age. Nine-year-olds worry about their weight. What I am getting to here is that there are some medical conditions, anorexia and bulimia, that are real and are happening to younger people. The pressure to fit in is great. That is why I encourage you to include her parents in on this discussion. They need to be aware of the possibilities of these illnesses occurring. Here is another opportunity for you to have a meeting with the parent to discuss the child. Being a "child care mom" is a very important job! Let me know how this one develops.

Playing with Food

Q

Dear Nurse Libby,

Linda, age three, has recently started playing with her food. She pulls whatever it is into tiny pieces and then she pours it off the plate onto the table or the floor, even with food she likes to eat. At first, I tried to downplay the behavior because all the other kids were making such a big deal about it. I told her that I do not need an extra mess to clean up and needed her help in keeping the kitchen clean. She seemed to understand what I said, and when she asked me if I was mad at her, I told her that I was not angry but that I was sad because of the extra work she had caused me.

With her next snack, she did the same thing. I don't think she is even aware that she is doing this. This may sound crazy, but she seems to be a little depressed or preoccupied lately. Could this be possible at her age? Please let me know your opinion.

A

Dear Mrs. Kathy,

Linda is too old for this behavior. Nine- to 12-month-olds play this game with food. It is a developmental milestone. They are realizing that things disappear and follow where they go. It is the game of throwing everything off the high chair table!

If she feeds herself, sitting at the table with the other children, and only behaves this way for snack time but eats regular meals, I wouldn't worry too much. I would not give her a snack! Either she is not hungry because she is not in a growth spurt, or she may not require as much food as another child right now. I would not worry, but make sure you do not reward this behavior.

Involve her in the cleanup process as well. Have her help with picking the food up off the floor or assist you with sweeping up the mess. This will help her realize that she needs to be careful while she is eating.

Q

Dear Nurse Libby,

I wanted to follow up with you about Linda throwing food on the floor. I discussed the issue with her mother, and she stated that they were having the same problem with Linda at home. I moved her high chair away from the other children, and the problem stopped. I guess she enjoyed the reaction from the other children, and once they could not see her, the food tearing lost its appeal.

A

Dear Mrs. Kathy,

I'm glad Linda's meal manners have improved! It could also be her age. She may be over the throw-things-off-the-high-chair stage. It may also be that she is in a growth spurt and is eating everything in sight. So throwing away food would not be an option at this time.

After you moved her high chair, she lost her audience. The test will be to move her back to the table. It is also a good idea, emotionally. We humans learn to eat socially if we are allowed to eat with other people. She needs to learn meal manners and to socialize with others at meal times. So, let her back at the table and see what happens.

Chapter 7

LETTERS ON CHILD CARE STRUCTURE

What to Look For in Child Care Providers

Q

Dear Mrs. Kathy,

Several of my patients have asked me what to look for when choosing a child care provider. I thought I would seek your help on answering this question.

A

Dear Nurse Libby,

This is an excellent question and actually one that I answer a lot. I have had a waiting list for several years, but I am always getting calls from people in search of child care. I like to give them suggestions on what to look for even though I cannot help them.

The first thing parents need to do is to contact their local child care administration and ask for a list of licensed child care providers and centers in their area. Parents should always choose a provider who is licensed because that person is supervised by the state. Educational requirements must be met, and a complete inspection of the home is part of the strict criteria required to become licensed.

Once parents have received this list, they should begin making some calls. A first impression is a lasting impression; so if parents do not feel comfortable with the provider on the phone, they need go no farther. They should simply and courteously end the conversation and move on to the next person on the list. Parents should be prepared with a list of questions that they would like to ask. A good thing for parents to remember is that no matter what time they call, the provider will probably be busy.

Some Questions to Ask

- *Are you licensed?*
- *Do you have any openings?*
- *What are your hours?*
- *What do you charge?*
- *How many children do you currently have in your program?*

- *Do you provide meals and snacks?*
- *Do you offer a contract?*
- *What are your vacation and closing policies?*
- *What kind of activities will my child participate in?*

If this provider or center meets parents' requirements, then it's time to set up an appointment for parents and their child to interview the provider. This appointment should be during business hours.

What to Look For

There are three main things to observe during the interview: the child care provider, the other children, and the condition of the center/home and its surroundings.

The Caregiver

- *What is your first impression? Do you feel comfortable with her/them?*
- *Does she (Do they) appear to have control over the children?*
- *Does she (Do they) appear to enjoy the children?*
- *Is the atmosphere relaxed?*
- *Does she (Do they) have a list of policies and a written contract?*
- *How does she (do they) interact with your child?*
- *What is the schedule of the day's events?*
- *What activities, crafts, and learning sessions are provided?*

The Other Children

- *Do the children appear to be relaxed and enjoying themselves?*
- *Are the children following a routine?*
- *How do the other children relate to your child?*

The Surroundings

- *Are the areas used for child care safe and clean?*
- *What is the condition of the toys that the children play with?*
- *Is there ample room for the children to play?*
- *Are there any pets or animals?*
- *What is the policy on smoking?*
- *Where do the children sleep and eat? Is this area clean?*

When the interview is completed, parents should ask themselves how they feel. If they are comfortable with the child care provider, they may have found the right place for their child. They should take a few days to listen to their instincts, but if they find that they are comfortable, they should call the provider or center to go back and discuss the contract agreement.

What to Look For in a Contract

It is the parents' responsibility to read and completely understand the contract before signing it. This will avoid any misunderstanding between parents and the child care provider or center.

The contract should contain:

1. *Hours of operation.*
2. *Amount due for service.*
3. *When payment is due.*
4. *Late fees for not picking the child up before closing time.*
5. *Late fees if payment is not made on time.*
6. *Meal policies.*
7. *Days the child care is closed, holidays, vacation, and the like.*
8. *Policies about bringing sick children to child care.*
9. *Type of notice needed to terminate the contract.*
10. *Agreement to transport children for field trips or to and from school.*

These are only a few examples of what may be in the contract agreement. Having a clear understanding of the policies and rules will start the relationship off on the right foot. Communication is very important to this relationship.

Child Care Contract Questions

Dear Nurse Libby,

I have taken the liberty to answer some of the most common questions that parents ask me in regards to child care contracts. I thought I would share them with you. First, these are the usual questions:

1. *Do I pay for a day of child care if my child is absent?*
2. *What is normal payment policy for vacation or closed days?*
3. *Should I notify my child care center/provider if my child will not be present for the day?*
4. *Should I pay a late fee if I do not pick my child up on time?*
5. *What is the policy on late payments to the provider/center?*
6. *If my child damages something, should I be required to pay for it?*
7. *Should the child care center/provider replace a lost or broken item that was brought from home?*

8. *What is the policy on allowing a sick child to enter the child care environment?*
9. *Why will my child care provider only give my child one dose of an over-the-counter medicine?*
10. *What is the policy on staying after hours to discuss issues regarding my child?*

Now to address each question individually.

1. **Should I pay for child care if my child is absent?**

   Most home as well as child care centers are allowed a certain number of children per day. For example, I am allowed eight children in my home at one time. When you sign a child care contract, you are actually signing up for one of the eight slots available. Each slot has a dollar value, which is how we budget our income. If we did not charge you when you did not come, we would lose money. It's like renting an apartment. When you go away on vacation you still pay for the apartment, even though you are not there.

2. **What is the normal payment policy for vacation or closed days?**

   As a home child care provider, I do take a paid vacation. I do, however, post my vacation weeks in advance. I encourage families to try to take that same week off because they have to pay for the week anyway. As far as weather-related closing, I am normally always open.

   Vacations in child care centers are usually not an issue because centers do not close. They hire extra staff or juggle schedules during summer months. If the weather becomes a concern, a center may need to close early or for the entire day. Discuss this policy with the director of the center before signing your contract. When signing a contract, be sure to read and discuss the vacation policy with your provider to avoid any confusion.

3. **Should I notify my child care provider/center if my child will not be present?**

   If your child is attending a home child care, I would suggest notifying the provider as soon as you realize that your child will be absent so that activities will not be held up waiting for your child to arrive. Child care centers have their own policies on absent children, so review their guidelines. Do not assume that if you do not show up, you do not need to call. They may have plans for the day and are waiting on your child!

4. **Should I pay a late fee if I do not pick my child up on time?**

   Yes. On several occasions I have been late for school and church events, as well as softball games and cheerleading practice, waiting for a late parent to arrive. Each child care provider/center has a policy for lateness, and it is important to be aware of and follow it. My policy is that I close at a certain time, and I give my parents 15 minutes past that time to arrive. After that, I charge a fee of $1.00 per minute.

5. **What is the policy on late payments if I forget to pay my provider/center?**

   I normally charge a late fee of $10.00 per day for a late payment. I have found that when I charge a late fee, parents are more likely to remember to pay me.

   Child care centers also enforce late payment policies. It is important to discuss these policies prior to signing a contract.

6. **If my child damages something at the child care center, should I be required to pay for the damage?**

   If a child damages something while in my care, I discuss the situation with the parent. If I feel that the child was old enough to know better and that the damage resulted in something that was not an accident, then I may have the child pay back his debt by helping me with extra chores.

   Most centers are childproof, but occasionally something will be damaged. Again, it depends on the age of the child and the reason the damage occurred. The contract may state that you are responsible to repair or replace the item.

7. **Should the child care provider/center replace a lost or broken item that was brought from home?**

   There are several reasons why I do not allow children to bring things to the child care center from home.

- *It will be broken.*
- *It will get lost.*
- *Other children will fight over it.*

In my contract, it states that I will not be responsible for anything brought from home except the child. I will allow a special animal or blanket at nap time, but I do not promise that it will not get lost.

Most centers have the same type of policy as I do. Some centers allow nothing to be brought from home. Please read your contract so that you understand their policy.

8. **What is the policy on allowing a sick child to enter the child care environment?**

   A sick child needs to be home in bed getting lots of extra love and care. I cannot take the time to give a child the extra attention needed while effectively caring for the other children in my home.

   When a child arrives sick, he or she is spreading germs to other children as well as to me. If I become sick, then I may need to close.

   Child care centers are also very strict on permitting sick children into their care. The state has certain guidelines that both home and child care centers must follow. You may want to discuss these guidelines when you are signing your contract.

9. **Why will my child care provider only give one dose of an over-the-counter medicine?**

   Each state has a set of guidelines for administering medicine. In Maryland, we are allowed to give only one dose of an over-the-counter medicine, unless written permission is given by a health care provider. The reason for this is to encourage parents to take the child to their health care provider. A cough for a week could be bronchitis. This rule keeps illnesses to a minimum. For questions concerning the rules in your state, contact your local health department.

   Some child care centers and providers will refuse to administer any medication at all. Please make sure that you are familiar with your provider's policies.

10. What is the policy on staying after hours to discuss issues regarding my child?

I give each parent a report of the activities of the day at the time of pick up. I feel it is important to discuss all issues when they occur. If, however, the parent is running late or the issue needs to be discussed at length, I may suggest that I call the parent later in the evening.

Child care centers may have different policies as far as staying open late to discuss an issue with a parent. They may ask you to set up a meeting or arrive earlier so that they have the time needed for a detailed account of your child's day. It is a good idea to discuss closing policies prior to signing a contract.

Index

C

D

E

I

J

L

R

S

Y

Z